The Buddha in You

Also by Lama Lhanang Rinpoche
and Mordy Levine

The Tibetan Book of the Dead for Beginners:
A Guide to Living and Dying

The Beginner's Guide to Karma: How to Live
with Less Negativity and More Peace

The Buddha in You

A BEGINNER'S GUIDE TO BUDDHISM, FROM KARMA TO NIRVANA

Lama Lhanang Rinpoche
and Mordy Levine

sounds true
BOULDER, COLORADO

Sounds True
Boulder, CO

The excerpt by Roshi Joan Halifax was reprinted from *How Do You Pray?: Inspiring Responses from Religious Leaders, Spiritual Guides, Healers, Activists, and Other Lovers of Humanity*, edited by Celeste Yacoboni, by permission of Monkfish Book Publishing Company, Rhinebeck, New York.

Published 2025

Cover and jacket design by Rachael Murray
Book design by Meredith Jarrett

Printed in the United States of America

BK07178

Library of Congress Cataloging-in-Publication Data

Names: Lama Lhanang, Rinpoche, author. | Levine, Mordy, author.
Title: The Buddha in you : a beginner's guide to Buddhism, from Karma to
    Nirvana / Lama Lhanang Rinpoche and Mordy Levine.
Description: Boulder, CO : Sounds True, [2025] | Includes bibliographical
    references.
Identifiers: LCCN 2024041325 (print) | LCCN 2024041326 (ebook)
    | ISBN 9781649633798 (paperback) | ISBN
    9781649633804 (ebook)
Subjects: LCSH: Buddhism.
Classification: LCC BQ4022 .L353 2025 (print) | LCC
    BQ4022 (ebook) | DDC 294.3—dc23/eng/20241209
LC record available at https://lccn.loc.gov/2024041325
LC ebook record available at https://lccn.loc.gov
    /2024041326

FSC
www.fsc.org
MIX
Paper | Supporting
responsible forestry
FSC® C103096

Dedication of Merit

May all beings become omniscient and attain
Buddhahood, defeating all faults and enemies!

May all beings disturbed by waves of birth, old age, sickness,
and death be liberated from the ocean of cyclic existence!

"Enjoy this moment with wisdom, compassion and kindness . . . We all have the chance to be a Buddha one day."

—Lama Lhanang

Contents

1

Why Buddhism?

When we meet people who ask about Buddhism, these are some of the most common reasons they are curious about this path. Some of these reasons might be yours:

- Many people have a perception that Buddhists are calm, quiet, peaceful people, and they find this attractive.

- Their life has not turned out the way they expected, and they hope that Buddhism will help them find the path to get back on track.

- They heard about or tried meditation and think that might make them happy. They might think, "Once I start meditating, I am sure my life will be better."

- They recognize that they are living with anxiety or fear. It is uncomfortable. They look around and think the Buddhist path will somehow eliminate or reduce the intensity of those feelings.

- They encountered the Dalai Lama on social media, through one of his books or courses, or in the news, and are inspired by his persona.

It seems like he is one of the happiest people on Earth. And somehow, they feel that this man has the answers they are looking for. They want to be more like him.

- They observed that the Buddhists they know don't think or view life like most other people.

- They read that one of their favorite actors or actresses practice Buddhism and are curious.

- They keep reading profound quotes by "the Buddha" on mugs, napkins, or Instagram, and it sure sounds like he knew a lot about life's toughest issues.

Do any of these reasons resonate with you? What draws you to Buddhism? There are countless reasons people are inspired to learn about it. We are both devout Buddhist practitioners—Lama Lhanang has been a lifelong Buddhist, while Mordy became a Buddhist as an adult. We have both found this path to be profound, beautiful, and helpful, and we love to share it with anyone who is curious.

We wrote this book to share basic information about Buddhism with anyone who is interested—whether you have any intention of becoming Buddhist or not. People practice Buddhism in many different ways, and this short book can't cover them all. Instead, we aim to offer an overview of some of the key teachings of Buddhism. And since what draws many people to Buddhism is its contemplative nature, we also include reflection questions, meditations, or practices with each chapter. We encourage you to try them to get a flavor of the practice. But of course, you are welcome to skip them—please follow your instincts.

Many people begin to investigate Buddhism by reading about the Buddha who lived 2600 years ago. He was a man—not a god. And what he taught resonates with us.

And this generates more questions! How can I be like the Buddha? If the Buddha isn't a god, is Buddhism a religion? Who do Buddhists pray to? Is Buddhism a way of life, a philosophy, a science? We will answer some of these questions directly, and some we will leave up to you after you finish this book.

For many people, the religion we were born into didn't meet our needs, and in some cases may have even caused more harm than good. This can leave a void or confusion, which triggers our curiosity for other spiritual paths in life.

Many people have tried to meditate and sensed that there was something in the practice that needed more investigation. And after all, wasn't Buddhism the foundational inspiration for the mindfulness meditation we now see all over the world?

Many have heard that Buddhists have practices about how to die in peace. And even though you may not understand what Nirvana means, when we die, wouldn't it be nice to go there?

However you got to this moment, you are reading this book now. And we are very happy you're checking out this thing called Buddhism.

It is our desire that you will benefit from the teachings, practices, and explanations here. And we hope we can answer many of the questions that you may have about Buddhism as you begin to discover the Buddha in you!

Keep in mind, though, that sometimes asking questions leads to even more questions!

Contemplate

- What motivated you to pick up this book?
- What do you hope to get out of reading it?
- What does Buddhism mean to you right now?

Knowing your motivation will likely ensure that you find what you are looking for! You don't need to be a Buddhist to read this book or benefit from its contents. Feel free to take what works for you and leave the rest.

2

Who Was the Buddha?

S iddhartha Gautama was born into a wealthy family in approximately 563 BCE, in what is now Nepal. His father was the chief of the state of Shakya, located in the foothills of the Himalayas. In many prayers and chants you may see his name written as Buddha Shakyamuni, which literally means "enlightened one who is sage of the Shakyas."

His mother died soon after giving birth to Siddhartha. He was raised by his father and his aunt, who eventually became his stepmother. His father, like many parents, did his best to shield Siddartha from all human sorrow. But one day, curiosity got the best of Siddhartha.

He left his family's palatial home to see what life was like for those outside of his cushy, opulent environment. While being driven around by his charioteer, he observed what for him were unusual sights—an older man, an ill man, and the corpse of someone who had died. When his charioteer explained to him that this is what everyone experiences in life, he was greatly surprised.

On his way back to the palace, Siddhartha saw an ascetic monk walking peacefully. The human suffering that he saw that day, juxtaposed with the image of someone who knew how to find peace in the world, awoke something in him. It triggered in him a desire to seek the meaning of life.

Soon after, while still in his twenties, Siddhartha left his wealthy family—including his new wife and child—to try to understand why people suffer. For some readers of history, leaving one's wife and child to search for liberation or awakening can be viewed in a negative light. However, this act can also be viewed as a courageous and selfless act. Siddhartha left the comfort of a palace, searching for awakening so he could end suffering for all sentient beings—including his wife and child. We see this as truly an act of selflessness.

He spent years as a wandering ascetic, meditating and studying with many teachers and practicing with yogis. Ascetics are people who practice severe self-discipline for religious purposes. But he was not able to find liberation from suffering for himself or for others. He was dissatisfied with this lack of progress. Determined to find the answers for himself, he left his teachers and embarked on his own path.

After six years of wandering, meditating, and living an ascetic lifestyle, he was still not able to make the progress he had hoped for. Underweight, exhausted, and physically spent, he decided to sit under a tree in Bodh Gaya, a town in the Indian state of Bihar, and vowed not to leave that spot until he attained liberation or awakening. After six days and nights, with great effort, focus, and concentration, he did!

One of the many realizations he attained as he became enlightened was the understanding that the path of extremes did not bring liberation. Asceticism put the body under severe conditions and only created enemies of the body and mind. The body is not separate from the mind. The body should not be punished. And the other extreme, desire cultivated by hedonism, only brought more desire. Neither extreme led to an enlightened state. His enlightened knowledge born of both extremes showed that the path of the middle way was the best path to reduce suffering and to liberation.

A story best illustrates this idea. The Buddha was asked by one of his new students, a highly skilled lute player, why he was having difficulty meditating. Buddha asked his student, "When playing the lute, what happens when the strings of the lute are too tight?" His student responded easily, "The strings will break." And when he asked his student, "What happens when the strings of the lute are too loose?" his student responded, "Well, then the lute won't play." His student immediately understood that meditation was similar. The middle way—for both meditation and one's approach to life, thoughts, and decisions—was the path toward a peaceful mind and enlightenment.

After achieving his enlightened state of mind, the Buddha wandered the countryside, taught whoever requested teachings, and accumulated many devoted followers. The aura of enlightenment that surrounded him did not go unnoticed. When meeting people, many observed this bright countenance and asked him who he was. His response was simply,

"I am Buddha." The word Buddha means awakened, or one who has become aware.

For the rest of his life, the Buddha wandered through Northern India, teaching anyone who expressed interest in reducing their suffering or seeking liberation. He also created an order of monks and nuns, who lived according to his teachings. He ensured that they spread the teachings far and wide for generations to come.

The Buddha passed away in approximately 483 BCE, at the age of 80. It is thought that his students numbered in the thousands before he died. Today, there are more than 500 million Buddhists around the world.

The Buddha's realizations after his enlightenment included the understanding of many aspects of life. They include karma, impermanence, suffering, the central importance of compassion for all sentient beings, and an understanding of how what we call the "self" truly exists. We look forward to sharing the Buddha's teachings on these topics in upcoming chapters.

Contemplate

The story of Buddha is typically recounted with him leaving the palace of his father seeking to learn what was going on outside his sheltered life. Undoubtedly, prior to his enlightenment, his thoughts, actions, and speech were not always pure and serene.

As the story is told, he achieved enlightenment after years of practice and study.

The path was not easy for him, and the same may be true for you.

- Where and why did your spiritual path start?
- What have you learned so far on your path?
- Where do you think this path will take you?

3

The Evolution of Buddhism

S ince the Buddha's lifetime, his teachings have spread
around the world. And in that process, Buddhism
became influenced by the cultures of the countries where it
flourished. As Buddhism evolved in each of these cultures,
variations developed, and interpretations of many of the
core tenets sometimes differed from culture to culture, and
country to country.

As in all religions, there are many different types of
Buddhist schools. Broadly speaking, many scholars identify three main schools of Buddhism: Theravada Buddhism,
Mahayana Buddhism, and Vajrayana Buddhism. In chapter
17, we will provide a brief description of each and explain
how they are similar and how they differ from each other.
Regardless of their differences, all Buddhists generally agree
on the teachings that are ascribed to Buddha himself.

In addition, great Buddhist masters since the Buddha's
time have emphasized various dimensions of the core
tenets to their students, depending on the students' needs
as well as their own proclivities. Many of these masters created commentaries of their own, which were written down

by their students and passed on to the next generations. Depending on the country, the culture, and the school, there may be a different emphasis on some of the core tenets we will be describing here.

Although we are both practitioners in Vajrayana Buddhism, over our lifetime we have enjoyed learning and practicing the different ways Buddhism is taught in all schools around the world, and we are excited to share them with you here.

If we wanted to keep this book even shorter than it already is, we could synopsize Buddhism in just a few words spoken by His Holiness the Fourteenth Dalai Lama. As one of the most well-known spiritual leaders of his country and culture, he has been known to describe Buddhism succinctly: "My religion is simple. My religion is kindness."

We hope that when you are done reading, you will not only have a sense of the different aspects of Buddhism, but also how they all interrelate with each other. Every topic that we visit is related to every other topic in this book. No one topic stands on its own by itself in a void. They are—as are our lives—all interrelated.

Contemplate

Your core values have likely developed over time and may be very different now than years ago.

- How would you describe your core values?
- How did they develop over time?
- Does the Dalai Lama's description of Buddhism resonate with your core value? Why or why not?

The Four Noble Truths

The Buddha's first teachings after attaining enlightenment were given to five of his former spiritual companions, ascetics he had practiced with for years as a wanderer prior to his liberation.

Upon meeting up with the Buddha after his achievement, these ascetics were upset to see their former companion eating food like a normal person. They expected him to be abstaining and going hungry as he had previously. They thought he had abandoned the spiritual path and initially shunned him. But they could not ignore the aura of enlightenment that surrounded him!

The very first teachings he gave them, which are the basis of all Buddhist teachings, are known as the Four Noble Truths. These teachings are also known as the First Turning of the Wheel of Truth (Dharma), which refers to a "revolution" in how we can view the world.

The First Noble Truth:
The Truth of Suffering

The Sanskrit word used to describe suffering is *dukkha*. However, *dukkha* can also be translated as disappointment, struggle, dissatisfaction. Many of us don't feel like we suffer, as the word is commonly understood, until something unexpectedly bad happens! Other people might feel like life itself is suffering, as we experience and witness so much pain in the world. Keeping in mind these other translations helps us have a fuller understanding of dukkha and suffering.

As humans, we experience dissatisfaction when our circumstances change and something happens that we don't want, or we want something that doesn't happen! We can all relate to this aspect of our lives. Our disappointment can refer to minor, inconsequential things (for example, the restaurant doesn't have my favorite pancakes on the menu anymore) to situations of great consequence (for example, a loved one is dying or ill). Birth, illness, aging, and death, all unavoidable experiences for all sentient beings, involve pain and suffering.

In essence, the Buddha is saying that when we experience undesirable changes in our lives, we don't like it. And these experiences can trigger challenging states of mind, such as annoyance, irritation, anger, jealousy, grief, and more.

The Second Noble Truth: The Cause of Suffering

The Second Noble Truth says that suffering just doesn't show up out of nowhere. It has a cause, which we can identify.

Suffering is triggered by an event, person, thing, experience, or even sometimes just a thought that pops into our mind.

These triggers can be identified as craving. We crave sensual pleasures and crave not to have unpleasant experiences. We crave for things to go the way we want them to go. We crave to stay alive! We crave for things to change when we don't like how they are going or crave for them to remain unchanged if we do.

The Third Noble Truth: The Cessation of Suffering

More good news is that we can put a stop to much of our suffering. Just as suffering has a cause, there is also a way to end it. We don't have to live with dukkha—disappointment, struggle, and challenging states of mind. We can be free from suffering.

This is the Buddha's promise—it is truly a powerful teaching. And we also acknowledge the profound suffering many of us live with, from experiencing violence to receiving a devastating health diagnosis. Indeed, the Buddha taught that we can be free from our cravings, but he did not teach that we can omit all difficulty in our lives.

Healing from trauma takes time, care, and support. We and countless other practitioners have found that the Buddhist mindset can offer immense benefit, and we also want to make clear that it's not a magic wand.

The Fourth Noble Truth: The Eightfold Path

The Fourth Noble Truth gives us a road map to eliminating or minimizing suffering. It is a list of eight actions that we can follow. They are succinctly known as right view, right intention, right speech, right action, right livelihood, right effort, right mindfulness, and right concentration.

You may also see them categorized as follows:

- Ethics (right speech, right action, right livelihood)
- Meditation (right effort, right mindfulness, right concentration)
- Wisdom (right intention, right view)

As we go through this book, you will begin to see how these eight actions of body, speech, and mind work together to bring us to liberation, freedom from craving, and elimination of suffering.

Right View
Understanding karma (that our actions of body, speech, and mind have consequences—more on this in chapter 8), understanding the Four Noble Truths, and understanding

impermanence (that all things are constantly changing—more on this in chapter 5).

Right Intention
Having an attitude of kindness to others. Renunciation of actions of body, speech, and mind that cause harm to ourselves and others.

Right Speech
No lying. No gossip. No speech that harms or demeans others, and no sowing discord.

Right Action
No actions that cause harm to other people, including killing, stealing, or sexual misconduct. In our view, sexual misconduct refers to any sexual activity that does harm of any kind to another being.

Right Livelihood
Traditionally, this means pursuing work that contributes to the well-being of others and the world. Right livelihood also means avoiding work that causes harm to others, which might include arms trading, breeding animals for slaughter, or killing any sentient beings.

Right Effort
Awareness of one's mind, and working to control one's mind by reducing or eliminating negative thoughts and developing positive thoughts.

Right Mindfulness

Being aware of one's body, senses, feelings, and thoughts, including an acknowledgment of impermanence.

Right Concentration

Developing your mind through meditation. The intention is to train the mind to better understand compassion and the wisdom of realizing emptiness, impermanence, and suffering.

Many Buddhists meditate on the Four Noble Truths or on the Eightfold Path to absorb their teachings on a deeper level. We will visit meditation practices in more depth in chapter 11.

And how do you know what actions, thoughts, or speech either create suffering or can be used to eliminate it? The Buddha addressed this issue by saying, "Don't rely on me." Test it for yourself. You decide. In his words from the Jnanasara-samuccaya, "As the wise test gold by burning, cutting, and rubbing it (on a piece of touchstone), so are you to accept my words after examining them and not merely out of regard for me."

And more specifically, the Buddha said in the Kalama Sutra (AN 3:65) that if you test the teachings, or the belief systems that you are currently following, and they lead to your suffering or the suffering of others, give them up!

> When you know for yourselves that "these
> teachings are unskillful; these dharmas are
> blameworthy; these dharmas are criticized by

the wise; these dharmas, when adopted and carried out, lead to harm and to suffering"— then you should abandon them . . .

When you know for yourselves that "these teachings are skillful; these dharmas are blameless; these dharmas are praised by the wise; these dharmas, when adopted and carried out, lead to welfare and to happiness"—then you should enter and remain in them.

And finally, the Buddha used a metaphor for himself and his teachings. He referred to himself as the doctor who is there to diagnose illness and provide a remedy. When listening to his teachings (known as the Dharma), here is what he said in the Gandavyuha Sutra:

Noble one, think of yourself as someone who
is sick,
Of the Dharma as the remedy,
Of your spiritual friend as skillful,
And of diligent practice as the way to recovery.

Contemplate

- How do you relate to the concept of suffering, defined as when we can't always have what we want, or when we lose what we want to keep?

- What examples do you have in your life where you couldn't get what you really wanted, or lost what you really wanted to keep?

- What was your reaction? How did you feel? How long did it last? How did you recover?

- How would you approach that situation again should it arise? How can you test that new strategy to see if it works?

- If you could go back in time, what thoughts or actions did you have that created the environment or conditions that led to the suffering you experienced?

- Which aspects of the Eightfold Path feel right to you? Do any of them feel easy or hard to follow? No need to rush to answer. Take a few minutes to feel your reaction.

5

Emptiness and Impermanence

When we look around, we see a lot of solid things around us. Some are physical—we see buildings, cars, houses, people, nature, animals, and the list goes on. Some things aren't physical but also appear to be solid—relationships, financial situations, the world order, and more. We see things that we believe are solid and, to some degree, permanent. We typically don't see a house dissolve or fall apart in front of our eyes. In fact, when we enter a building, we rely on that building being solid, so that we can enter, inhabit, and exit it safely.

Logically we realize that at some point in time, those buildings, houses, and cars will no longer exist the way we see them exist now. They will change. They will change into something else—landfill, recycled materials, a renovated structure, or fall apart over a long period of time. Even though we logically know that most things change in time, when we see it, suddenly we are shocked. For example, when we saw the World Trade Center come down on 9/11, people around the world were shocked. We were shocked of course due to the immense loss of life, but some part of us was shocked because we viewed those physical structures as the epitome of solidity.

Those of us unfortunate enough to have lived in a war zone see this dissolution and change daily. One moment your house or a neighbor's house is there; the next moment it is not. One moment you or a loved one is healthy and going about daily life; the next moment they are not.

And this change is true in peaceful times as well. Cars slowly fall apart. Houses are taken down to make room for new houses, or we renovate. Children get older. Our preferences and opinions change. Termites eat away at structures. Governments change. Our bodies become ill or injured. We all change as we grow older.

When Buddhists refer to this phenomenon, we say, "All conditioned things are empty of *inherent* existence." This is a fancy way of saying that when we look at any "thing," it is made up of various parts that have come together to form that "thing" for a time (conditioned). And those parts came together (for a time) to create something that eventually will not be there anymore. So we say that "thing" does not "inherently" exist. It *appears* to exist in a solid, permanent way (inherent existence) but it is not. We cannot and should not grasp, desire, or take refuge 100 percent on any (conditioned) thing as being permanent. This is what we refer to in Buddhism as the teachings on Emptiness.

That does not mean we should have the expectation that at any given moment something we regard as permanent will fall apart. Yes, we can trust to go into an office building and transact business there or live in our homes safely.

But we can also remind ourselves that anything that comes together at some point will change.

Younger people rarely think about getting older or death. Sometimes we feel like we will continue to live exactly as we are at any given moment—healthy, unchanged—seemingly "forever." When the first gray hair pops up, or the first sign of balding or a wrinkle is noticed, we might be shocked and, for some of us, disheartened. We may even attempt to resist that inevitable march toward aging and death by coloring our hair or wearing our hairstyle differently to cover a balding area.

In some sense we can rely on what appears to be solid, so we can go about our lives in a "normal" way. But in another sense, we can also understand and not be surprised when things around us change. That is normal, and inevitable. As we understand this at deeper levels and embody this mentality, we are more likely to accept change as it goes on around us—whether we like it or not.

Many people feel that the teachings of Emptiness create feelings of uncertainty or unsteadiness about their lives. In fact, Emptiness means that anything and everything is possible. Nothing is set in stone. The teachings on Emptiness describe the reality that there is great potential for anything to happen!

This understanding is known as the wisdom of Emptiness.

Contemplate

"Life is very brief. Also, its length is unpredictable. If
you realize that you don't have that many more years
to live, and if you live your life as if you actually had
only one day left, then the sense of impermanence
heightens that feeling of the preciousness and gratitude."

—Pema Chödrön

- Can you identify times in your life when you
  expected a person, place, or thing to always be
  in your life—until they weren't?

- What did you feel when they were no longer
  around?

- If you were aware of the teaching of
  impermanence before they "disappeared," would
  you have appreciated their presence more?

6

Does the Self Exist?

Before we answer the question "Does the self exist?" we need to ask, exactly what is the "self"?

Is it my physical body? My brain? My mind? The combination of those things? Or is the "self" how I *view* myself?

However we define "self," we can all agree that the thing we call *self* is always changing. It is literally changing from moment to moment. We don't see or feel cells changing in our body, but we know they are. So although we don't see it from moment to moment or day to day, we know and experience our physical bodies changing over time.

And even our minds change from moment to moment. One moment I think I am so smart, and then the next moment I realize I was wrong. One moment I am angry with someone, and the next moment I am not. I think someone is my friend, and then they take advantage of me. Our mind changes its opinions and preferences more often than we realize. When I learn something new, my mind changes. When new thoughts pop in and out of my mind, my mind changes.

So Buddhists don't say, "The self does not exist." Anyone who says that hasn't been punched in the face! What we can say is that the self exists, just not in the way we may think.

The self is not a permanent object. To those who think our spirit or soul is a permanent phenomenon that continues to our next lifetime, Buddhists would say, "Yes, something does continue on to another lifetime, but it is not a permanent self." We would say that what does continue to the next lifetime is our karma and consciousness. But that too changes from moment to moment.

Another way to view karma, which we describe in more detail in chapter 8, is that karma refers to the habits of how we view ourselves, habits developed over our lifetime(s).

We create habits when we tell ourselves stories about who we are—stories about our opinions and our preferences. The stronger our preferences and the more we convince ourselves that we are "right" about something, the more this creates negative karma.

The more open-minded we are, the kinder and wiser we will be. When we are without strong preferences or judgments, that leads to kindness and wisdom, which creates positive karma. We form these opinions and judgments about ourselves, others, and the world we inhabit on a daily basis.

She is so bossy.

I am really smart.

The restaurant staff here is always rude.

You are always mean.

I am one of the best employees.

I am a good mother.

She will never understand.

That religion is so violent.

That leader doesn't know what he is talking about.

Democrats/Republicans are always _____

As we tell ourselves stories about ourselves or others repeatedly, they become factualized in our minds. They are no longer opinions. In this way we prop up the self, and because of repetition and factualization we think our self is unchanging and permanent.

And in the face of anything that threatens that sense of self (for example, when we find out we were wrong about our strong opinion), we experience the result of that negative karma. We experience irritation, annoyance, anger—challenging states of mind.

What about war? We all agree that war is a horrible thing to be avoided or eliminated at all costs. Are we allowed to feel strongly about it? Doesn't it make sense to have a strong opinion about it? In some sense, yes. We can feel strongly about situations that help reduce the suffering of others. And we can also simultaneously have compassion for all parties involved since they are all suffering. These thoughts don't prop up the self.

The good news is we can change how we relate to the idea of our self, to reduce this suffering. We look forward to sharing how in chapter 11, "Meditation," and chapter 12, "Tools to Change Our Habits."

Practice

Here is a simple way to reduce the strong sense of self that encourages our selfishness, which in turn leads to dissatisfaction or unhappiness.

- Pick any group, species, race, or gender, and in your own words, create a prayer that wishes them well. It can be short, even just one or two sentences. Then recite it slowly a few times.

- How do you feel when you're wishing others well?

7

Interdependence

Buddhists believe that we are all—in some way, shape, or form—interdependent with one another. This means we are all connected to each other in some way. No one lives in a vacuum.

The apple you ate today was grown by a farmer, trucked to a market near you, stocked on the shelf by a stock person, sold to you by a cashier, carried home with you perhaps in a car that is powered by gas or electricity from a utility, built by many people who worked for a car manufacturer.

If we wanted to be more comprehensive and go back even further, we would see that the farmer was taught how to farm by their parents or someone they worked for on the farm. Parents were responsible for bringing that farmer into the world as a baby, raising them, and training them to be the farmer that grew your apple!

The causes and effects are *infinite* in every direction. Not sure? How far can you go back in time? Without any one of those infinite influences, however minor, the food we eat may not have existed, or would exist differently. We could go back in time and uncover infinite causes or interdependencies associated with each step that had to take place before you ate that simple apple.

As such, we are reliant on others, and they are reliant on us. This understanding teaches us how we are truly all connected.

The COVID-19 pandemic is once again proof of our connectedness. The speed with which the infectious coronavirus traveled from person to person, and then country to country, was astonishing. The effects of climate change, also felt in every corner of the world, are caused by companies, people, or countries on one side of the earth, but impact the entire earth and its habitants. Sometimes immediately, and in most cases for years to come.

What can we learn from this?

We are all related. We all impact each other. The effects of our body, speech, and mind on others and the world we live in are infinite. This is a great opportunity for us. If we can live with love and awareness, it impacts others, and we are on our way to being Buddhas! As changes like these happen quickly, the golden rule—*Treat others as you would like to be treated*—may hold greater meaning than previously thought.

One of the first teachings that the Buddha's earliest students passed on to others is known as "Ye Dharma Hetu." The simple concept of interdependence that we have been discussing is taught in these short four lines, known as the Mantra of Interdependence. Its essence is that everything that arises has a cause.

Ye Dharma Hetu

Of those things that arise from a cause,

The Buddha has told the cause,
And also what their cessation is:
This is the doctrine of the Great Spiritual Being.

Contemplate

At your next meal, ask yourself or those you are dining with:

- Where did the meal come from?
- How did it get to your table?
- What people were involved in bringing this food to you? What were their tasks?
- How far back can you trace the food nourishing you?

8

Karma

Karma literally means "action." Karma can refer to actions of body, speech, or mind that we perform ("You are creating good karma by doing that"), or the consequences that we experience ("You missed the train because of your karma").

Karma is known as the law of cause and effect. On a very simple level, many people believe that this is what is intended by phrases like "What goes around comes around," "You deserved that," or "That's just karma." And to some degree, those phrases are true. However, karma is so much more complex than what's conveyed by those simple phrases.

Karma is based on one's intention or motivation behind an action of body (physically doing something), speech, or thought. Karma results from actions we do, say, or think. We refer to all of them as actions.

Motivation can be either selfless or selfish (or a combination of the two). My motivation to write a check to a nonprofit organization can be selfish (I want to impress my colleagues) or selfless (I want to help the unhoused people that are served by the organization). If you are helping low-income children because you have compassion and want to improve their lives, you are creating good karma. If you are angry with someone and yell at them, and you want to hurt them or show them that you are right, that would be a selfish motivation, creating negative karma. Note—it is not about whether you are right or wrong!

And of course, in most situations, there is a mixture of motivations that underlie action, speech, or thought. And the consequence of any of those actions can be experienced by the person doing the action immediately, or over time.

Any action you perform will result in consequences that you will experience in one or more of the following three ways:

1. The way that you impact someone else will happen similarly to you. For example, if you cheat someone out of five dollars, at some point in time someone will cheat you in a similar way. If you insult or offend someone verbally, at some point in the future someone will do the same to you.

2. You are more likely to "commit" that action again. You are establishing a habit. For example, if you are used to handling situations verbally (e.g., yelling) or physically (e.g., hitting), in the future the likelihood is that you will continue to handle those situations in the same way.

3. You are likely to find yourself in the same environment or situation again in the future. For example, if you are in a situation where it is okay not to clean up, to leave dirty dishes and clothes unattended, you are more likely to be in that type of environment in the future.

The consequences of our actions (karma) can be realized in the next moment, later in this life, or in future lifetimes (for those of us who believe in rebirth).

On a more subtle and more powerful level, as indicated in chapter 6 ("Does the Self Exist?"), karma is a habit of mind. When your mind repeats stories to itself about who you think you are, those views, preferences, and opinions become ingrained in your mind. Over time, you start to accept them as "fact."

For example: you might tell yourself that you are a great doctor and an on-time person. And when a person, situation, or reality arises that conflicts with your "facts," you experience challenging states of mind. You become angry when your patient, boss, or colleague says you are not a good doctor. Or when your wife insists you are late all the time (even though you were only two minutes late!).

Negative karma arises from the habituation of stories we tell ourselves, which we hold onto (dearly) as fact. We hold onto these stories, views, and preferences as "the way things are." When we were younger, these stories helped us to survive. These views supported our sense of self. But as they become factualized, they may no longer serve us well.

It is easier to retell ourselves these stories repeatedly than it is to observe and reflect a more accurate, changing reality. In some ways it can be comforting—until reality proves our stories wrong. How we feel and react when that happens is an example of suffering that comes from our tight grasp on our "selves."

Existing in this close-minded manner is regarded as an action (of mind) and creates negative karma. These habits of mind set us up for experiencing challenging states of mind. The more we hold onto these stories as facts, the greater the upset (suffering) when we are proven wrong by reality.

Being open-minded takes an incredible amount of bravery. That would require us to realize that anything is possible.

Vanilla ice cream is not *the* best; it's just different.

My colleague spoke with me offensively—not necessarily to harm me, but he may have been having a bad day.

Republicans/Democrats are not horrible people. They are just people with different experiences that have led to different opinions.

If you want good karma, train yourself to become more open-minded about how you view the world, your opinions, and second-guessing others' motivations. Know the difference between fact and opinion.

All our opinions and preferences about the world and other people's motivations are only guesses, based on our past experiences and biases. The real fact is that the possibilities of what reality might be are more nuanced and infinite than we think.

We create our own karma by how we think, speak, and act. It is up to us. Not up to Buddha or anyone else.

Contemplate

As mentioned above, your motivation determines whether you are creating good karma or bad karma. As you go through your day and make decisions—simple or complicated—ask yourself:

- What is my motivation behind this decision?
- Is my motivation purely selfish, purely selfless, or some combination of the two?
- If it is purely (or mostly) selfish, how can I change my motivation or decision to be more selfless?

9

The Present Moment

In the past several decades, the mindfulness movement in the West has grown exponentially. Mindfulness is now a common term used to refer to paying attention to the present experience, including thoughts, bodily sensations, and emotions. By doing so, we can reduce stress and anxiety in our lives. The mindfulness movement has helped many people in this regard.

At its most superficial level, if you can train your mind to be in the present moment, then it is not thinking about the past or the future. When we review the past, it is usually in the sense of, *I wish that had happened differently*. And when we try to predict the future and what it holds for us, it is usually identifying and highlighting the negative possibilities.

Lama Lhanang is known for teaching the following about the present moment: "The past is history. The future is mystery. The present moment is a gift."

The past is gone. There is nothing we can do about it. We certainly can't change it. So, there is no need to ruminate over it. "Shoulda woulda coulda" conversations with ourselves about the past are harmful stories we review in our mind repeatedly. In fact, they cause us stress and anxiety. They are counterproductive.

If we learn from our past, then that can be productive. But when we review, judge, or wish things were done differently—repeatedly—we are only harming ourselves. The stress, disappointment, annoyance, and anger we dredge up by reviewing the past in that manner is harmful.

And spending time worrying about the future? The future is unknown. There are a myriad number of possibilities about what the future holds. We can't predict it. And although it is good to plan, planning is different than worrying about it, or reviewing worst-case scenarios of what might happen. Those types of conversations we have with ourselves cause stress and anxiety. And they prevent us from planning appropriately. We end up making decisions or plans driven by fear or anxiety, instead of clear, sensible views about how to prepare for the future.

When we can train our mind to be in the present moment, we are no longer entangled in the past or future. In fact, it is impossible to think about the past or the future if you are truly in the present. The mind cannot be in the present moment and think about the past or future at the same time.

We can be in the present moment by observing ourselves—our thoughts, emotions, and physical sensations—at any time we choose.

In addition, being in the present moment can be calming to the mind. It slows down the chatter in our mind, which can be noisy, confusing, and upsetting. In the clear mind of the present, we can make better decisions. We can see and interact with the people and world around us with greater clarity. Without fear of the future or regretting the past, we find it easier to be giving, open-minded, generous, and generally nicer people to ourselves and others!

Sounds great! Except that for most of us, being in the present moment does not come naturally. We are habituated to think thousands of thoughts in any given day. As children growing up, our family and culture trained us to think about ourselves first. And later as adults, we continued to train ourselves to be self-centered—in our careers, relationships, desires, and decision-making. Of course, we do need to take care of ourselves, our health, and our families. So, there is a balance required to ensure we are not self-centered to the detriment of others.

This change in the mind's operating system to be calmer, more at peace, and less self-centered requires training in meditation. And although there are probably hundreds of different types of meditation in Buddhism, one of the most common beginner meditations is to follow your breath. Following your breath gradually retrains your mind to be in the present moment. It is a simple, powerful, and effective technique. And anyone can do it, anywhere and anytime.

We will provide the instructions for that meditation in more detail when we discuss meditation in chapter 11.

Practice

Try following your breath now for only two minutes!

- Set your timer for two minutes and then sit or rest in a way that feels comfortable to you. You can close your eyes or rest them with your eyes slightly open. Simply observe the air as it passes through your nostrils.

- No need to make any modifications. Just observe the air you are breathing in its most natural rhythm.

- If you find yourself getting distracted by sounds or thoughts, no problem. Just go back to observing the air passing through your nostrils.

Throughout the day when you get annoyed, irritated, or even bored, practice the same exercise and see how it feels. You can own it! Make it second nature.

10

Bodhicitta

The practice of Bodhicitta (pronounced bo-dee-chitta) is a primary theme that runs through all Buddhist practices in all Buddhist schools. Bodhicitta is a combination of two Sanskrit words. *Bodhi* means "awakened" or "enlightened," and *Citta* means "mind." "Enlightened mind" could be the two perfect words to describe the practice, goal, or direction that Buddhist practitioners aim to develop!

Bodhicitta can also be translated as Great Compassion.

Bodhicitta can be exemplified by two prayers that Buddhists recite before, during, or after a Buddhist practice. Many practitioners recite these prayers several times a day to immerse themselves in this wonderful teaching.

Zen Buddhists (a Mahayana school) recite the aspirational prayer "Four Great Vows" daily, and at the end of retreats or practices.

Four Great Vows
Sentient beings are numberless; I vow to save them.
Desires are inexhaustible; I vow to put an end to them.

The Dharmas are boundless; I vow to master them.
The Buddha Way is unattainable; I vow to attain it.

The concept of Four Immeasurables, or Four Brahmaviharas (Heavenly Abidings), is an important teaching in all schools of Buddhism. These qualities that we can cultivate are loving-kindness, compassion, appreciative joy, and equanimity.

Here is an example of this teaching in prayer form.

Four Immeasurables
May all beings have happiness and the causes of happiness.
May all beings be free from suffering and the causes of suffering.
May all beings rejoice in the well-being of others.
May all beings live in peace, free from greed and hatred.

The Four Immeasurables is such a beautiful and meaningful way to express Bodhicitta that it can be used as a stand-alone practice (by simply repeating it over and over), or as an introductory prayer for a meditation practice. What a beautiful way to set the tone for any spiritual or religious practice.

You may be starting to get the idea that Buddhism is all about reducing the suffering of sentient beings—including yourself! "All sentient beings" refers to all living beings, not just us humans. That's a lot of beings! Reducing suffering for all sentient beings is not an easy thing to digest, let alone do.

Many people naturally approach a religion or a way of life and ask, "What's in it for me?" It is a natural question to ask. From a Buddhist perspective, we seek "true" happiness, not just from money or sensual pleasures. And Buddhism teaches that the happiness we seek comes from the reduction or elimination of self-centered thoughts, speech, and actions.

We are then free—free from suffering—because we no longer cling to desires from our self-centered mentality. This freedom benefits others as we aspire and act for others to be without suffering as well. And it benefits oneself—we feel good when others are free of suffering. Conversely, lack of this freedom is harmful to us, and harmful to others.

Yes, each of us humans is a sentient being and we seek to reduce our own suffering for sure. And *the way we do that* is by helping others. As we go through each chapter, how that works will become clearer.

The Dalai Lama states this beautifully and succinctly:

> My advice is that if you must be selfish, be wisely selfish. Wise people serve others sincerely, putting the needs of others above their own. Ultimately you will be happier. The kind of selfishness that provokes fighting, killing, stealing, using harsh words, forgetting other people's welfare will only result in your own loss.

Mahatma Gandhi was once asked, "What would you do if a plane was flying over your ashram with the intention to bomb you?" His answer: "I would pray for the pilot."

Another way that Bodhicitta may be defined is the desire to become enlightened to bring all sentient beings to enlightenment.

Why enlightenment? What's so great about enlightenment?

As we've established, all sentient beings live their lives experiencing suffering, dissatisfaction, or disappointment. As mentioned earlier, this is typically when we don't get what we want or expect, or we get what we don't want. The enlightened state of mind is devoid of this suffering.

When we practice with the mind of Bodhicitta, we develop compassion for all sentient beings—those close to us and those we don't even know. We develop compassion for others when they experience suffering—from birth, illness, growing old, dying, unwanted change, or not getting what they desire.

Compassion for others takes us out of our self-centered mindset, where we strive to satisfy the needs and desires of "me" or "I." When life is about "me" or "I," this is a dualistic view. What is dualism? When the focus is on "me," it is in juxtaposition to everyone and everything else. This is dualistic thinking.

On the other hand, when life is about helping others, our sense of self diminishes. When you help feed people experiencing homelessness, you are not worried about most of the things you might ordinarily focus on. We are not subject to the suffering that results from living a life where satisfying "me" and "I" is the priority.

Why is suffering associated with the self-centered attitude?

When we believe the illusion that our lives, homes, loved ones, and situations will all stay exactly as they are now, we set ourselves up for disappointment or shock—suffering. As we've discussed, suffering is inevitable, given that everything in the world is subject to change—at any time.

Great spiritually enlightened beings (not just from Buddhism) live their lives to help others. They are living in the present. They are not grasping at what happened in the past or the future, wishing things were different. They have great compassion for others without the self-centered mentality.

Another description of Bodhicitta is the "nature of the mind." When we meditate, or spend time with an advanced Buddhist teacher, we can *feel* and understand their great love and compassion for others. We can feel their wisdom mind. In this case, wisdom refers to a deep understanding that everything is impermanent, and we are all related and interdependent. And when we can understand this type of wisdom, we are not surprised by changes that take place around us, even within ourselves. And as we see and feel interdependence, we naturally have compassion for others. They are just like us.

The self-centered mindset grasps and wishes for our lives and situations to be different when they don't go the way we hoped or expected. When we live with Bodhicitta, we don't have a mindset filled with desire to have more, or to have less. We are okay with the changes that we experience when life changes around us.

Things around us just "are," and we accept that. It doesn't mean we don't do our best to improve ourselves and the world, but we don't *add* a layer of additional grasping and clinging for things to be different.

The natural result when we reduce our self-centered mind is to feel, see, and understand that we are all made of the same material. We are all at heart (pun intended!) loving, compassionate, sentient beings.

The mind of Bodhicitta is so important that at the end of a service or prayer, many Buddhists express the desire to develop and spread Bodhicitta. They dedicate any merit they may have earned from the prayers, aspirations, or wishes just recited to the benefit of other sentient beings.

One dedication of this merit expresses the wish that Bodhicitta spreads far and wide among all sentient beings.

> Precious Great Compassion, the highest attitude,
> Where it is unborn, let it arise;
> Where it is born, let it never decline, but ever
>   increase,
> Rising higher, and higher!

In Buddhism, committed practitioners take vows, known as taking refuge. We will go into more depth on this in chapter 18. One of the lines in the refuge prayer is to take refuge in "Bodhicitta, the nature of the channels, wind, and essence." This strongly asserts that Bodhicitta nature is already within us—in the energy centers, channels, and space in our body. And as we remove our negative states of mind, what is left is pure compassion for ourselves and others, and the understanding of wisdom realizing Emptiness.

This aspiration to help reduce the suffering of others is certainly a practice that is preached and in many cases practiced by people of every religion on Earth. And we are so happy that that is the case. Bodhicitta is the core of Buddhism.

Practice

The Four Immeasurables prayer isn't reserved for Buddhist practitioners only. The ideas behind this prayer resonate with people of many religions as well as people of no religion at all.

- Try reciting the Four Immeasurables three times, bringing your best intention with every line.
  How do you feel while you are reciting them?
  How do you feel after?

11

Meditation

F or many Buddhists, meditation is their primary practice as they walk down the path seeking freedom. This
may seem overly simplistic, but gaining more control over
your mind is the best place to start. And meditation is a
straightforward way to do so.

As mentioned, there are many kinds of Buddhist meditation. There are different meditations for calming the mind,
concentrating, healing, connecting with a higher being,
praying, purification of our negative karma, and more.

For our purposes, here is an informal definition of meditation: any activity that can help to retrain the mind to be
calm, focused, and in control of how you think or feel.

Meditation can be sitting, walking, chanting, singing,
moving, lying down, standing, and more. Many activities
can fit this definition of meditation, *depending on what
you are doing with your mind at the time.* Walking while
thinking about solving your problems at work would not
fit this definition of meditation. Walking in the woods
and bringing your mind back to the present moment
when distracted would!

The meditation we will introduce here is simple, effective, and powerful to get you started.

First, we'll share two statements we believe to be true:

1. The only thing we can control in our lives is our state of mind.

2. The only thing that can give us freedom and long-term true happiness is our state of mind.

If you agree with these statements, even partially, then that can motivate you to learn and practice meditation. After all, we all want freedom and true happiness! Meditation is the most direct way to retrain our mind to reduce challenging states of mind—which will satisfy both statements one and two!

Let's revisit the triggers to our negative states of mind. When we say we are trying to regain control over our mind, what are we referring to?

We talked about the stories we tell ourselves in chapter 8, and how those stories are our opinions, preferences, and views that we tell ourselves about everything. And as we retell those stories repeatedly, they become mistaken as "fact," when they are not.

Over our lifetime this (mis)understanding becomes a habit. This is the habit of viewing ourselves, people, and situations in a fixed manner. The view of (mis)understanding reality. And together with this habit comes our reaction when the world around us shows us that we are mistaken. We react to any conflict with our personal stories and beliefs with annoyance, irritation, anger, jealousy, etc. And all coming from our mistaken thoughts!

We can be triggered to experience a negative mind state from an internal or external cause. Let's see how.

Internal Trigger

You are going about your day when suddenly, a judgmental thought about the past or a fearful thought about the future pops into your mind. And before you know it, your mind is reviewing the past or the future repeatedly. As a result, you are stressed, worried, angry. You were triggered internally, by a simple thought.

External Trigger

Another possibility is that something or someone external to you triggers you. External triggers can come from people (for example, "You forgot to get the milk from the store *again*?"); events ("We are going to have to lay you off today."); or situations ("I didn't realize my bank account balance was so low").

Now our habit is to react with an emotional or thought response (feeling angry, grumbling internally); physical reaction (drive faster than usual, take a swing at someone); or a reaction of speech ("How dare you fire me!").

Regardless of whether you are triggered internally or externally, these reactive responses are ingrained and have been so over many years.

It is now time to break these habits—our self-centered habit of how we view the world and ourselves, and the habit we developed from reacting unskillfully when triggered. The foundation that we will use to break these habits is meditation.

Through meditation, we start to retrain the mind to regain control over what it thinks, how it thinks, and when it thinks. And since these habits of mind have been around and ingrained for many years, as a child and then as an adult, it will take some time to retrain the mind.

A daily meditation practice builds the foundation. Then we can use other tools during the rest of our day (or night) for when we experience negative states of mind when triggered. We will look at these tools for the rest of our day in chapter 12, "Tools to Change Our Habits."

Sound simple? It can be, but only with a lot of practice.

But before we get too far down the road with the amazing powers and benefits of meditation, let's start at the beginning.

Your Meditation Environment

Find a quiet place and time for meditation. The area you choose to meditate should ideally be clean, light, uncluttered, special.

You can help your meditation environment feel special by adding flowers, a candle, photos of loved ones or beautiful places, natural objects that inspire you, statues, or other objects you enjoy.

And although we can meditate almost anywhere, when learning meditation, it is best to set ourselves up for success by following some of these suggestions.

Consider meditating before breakfast—before your day (and mind) is in full swing—but any time of day can work.

Use a timer with a light alarm tone so you can be consistent in your meditation time and know when to stop without having to check a clock.

Find any comfortable sitting position—on a chair, couch, cushion, or pillow—that will allow you to sit erect without too much or any discomfort. If sitting isn't feasible, you're welcome to meditate in any position that works for you.

Simple and Effective Meditation

Your posture should feel nice and tall. Not too relaxed, not slumped back, a relaxed-yet-alert posture.

Now read the following directions a few times, so when you are ready to start, you know what to do and you won't need to refer to them while meditating.

- Set your timer for ten minutes. If ten minutes feels daunting, any amount of time will do to start.
- Close your eyes.
- Observe your breath with no modification of the breath whatsoever.
- Observe the natural rhythm of your inhale and the natural rhythm of your exhale.

- Observe the air coming in and out of the nostrils.
- Then *after* each exhale, count in your mind (not out loud) a number, as follows:

    [Inhale exhale] one

    [Inhale exhale] two

    [Inhale exhale] three

    If/when you get to ten, go back to one and start again.

- You are not saying the words inhale/exhale.
- You are saying the number to yourself, not out loud, after your exhale.
- If at some point you notice that you are distracted by thoughts, sounds, or any distraction, no problem—just go back to observing your breath and start the count again with one.
- If you fall asleep and wake up, just go back to one.
- If you don't know what number you are on, no problem—just go back to one.

It is simple. But simple is not always easy! Try it!

What Now?

Start. Commit to once or twice a day. Good habits are hard to break.

Here is what you should expect each time you meditate: *no expectations whatsoever!*

Don't expect you will magically levitate, reach Nirvana, have control over your mind, see the future, become the calmest human being ever, be in bliss.

Just expect that by practicing meditation consistently, *over time*, you will receive the benefits. Even if you don't think you are doing it well, you will get the benefits.

What are the benefits?

- Peace of mind.

- The opportunity to decide how you want to respond when something unpleasant arises in your life.

- More awareness of your thoughts so you can see them coming before you get triggered.

- Over time, discursive thoughts running around in your mind will fade, and you will notice gaps in between thoughts. This is a sign that your mind is calming down.

- Greater ability to focus.

- You will be able to retrain your mind to concentrate, come back to the present moment more easily, have a better idea of what your mind is thinking, and reduce your stress level.

If you meditate for five or ten minutes a day, that is a very good start. Every day you meditate, you can give yourself an A grade! If you meditate twice in a day, you get an A+.

Here is a logical question you may be asking: "What if I am busy thinking the whole time? Why do I get an A?"

The amazing thing about meditation—which is misunderstood by many teachers and students alike—is that simply by sitting and doing the meditation described above, you get the benefits. Will you get them right away? Possibly, maybe some of them. The benefits we talk about accrue over time—*even if you aren't that good at it.*

Many people try to meditate, experience many thoughts, and conclude that they can't do it. Our habits weren't ingrained in a day, and they won't go away in a few meditation attempts. *They will go away over time.*

You will need to have trust and confidence that simply by doing it, you will get the benefits. No need to have any expectations for any one meditation session. You get the benefits by doing it, whether it feels that way or not.

It is like taking vitamins or starting a new workout routine. One vitamin is not going to make you feel healthier right away, but over time, it can. One short workout is not going to make you demonstrably stronger. But over time, it will.

Setting yourself up with expectations ("I heard meditation is amazing; I can't wait to feel the bliss") is setting yourself up for failure. Simply by doing it, you benefit. No judging, no expectations.

Now keep in mind that meditating five minutes a day will have a limited benefit on breaking habits that have been ingrained for so many years. If you are interested in starting a daily meditation practice, you can start at five or ten or fifteen minutes. But eventually at some point, if you are motivated after weeks or months, consider twenty minutes once a day on a consistent basis. This meditation practice is the foundation for the tools you will use during the rest of the day to be free of the habits you have created since you were born. Those tools are the contents of our next chapter.

Suffice it to say, the breathing meditation described above is all you need to get going—and possibly even for several years thereafter!

One of the amazing things about meditation is that whether you think you are doing it well or not, you still get the benefits! Of course, the more you do it, the greater the benefit. Many of us are quick to judge how well we are meditating, or for how long we are meditating. This is self-defeating and an inaccurate way to measure your efforts. We simply get the benefits by doing it.

Practice

You don't need to wait until you have twenty minutes carved out to try meditation. So, why wait?

- Let's do a two-minute version of the meditation as described above now—and see how it goes.

- Congratulations! It is that simple. We just do it. No expectations beforehand, and no judgments afterward. Next time, try five minutes!

- When done, silently say a short "thanks" to the great teachers who taught this meditation to their students over thousands of years.

The more we practice, the more the benefits accrue over time. Sometimes we feel calm immediately, and sometimes we may not. But over time, you will reap the rewards.

You now have this tool available to you 24/7, anytime, anywhere.

12

Tools to Change Our Habits

Why do I need additional tools if I am meditating once a day? Isn't that enough? No! For most of us, it's not.

If we want to break habits that we have developed over our lifetime, then fifteen to twenty minutes a day is a great start, but not enough. As mentioned, habits developed over a lifetime are hard to break.

We use the strength, calm, sensitivity, patience, and flexibility that we develop from our daily meditation to support us in implementing the tools described in this chapter. For many of us, that is where the rubber meets the road.

Sitting in the quiet, peaceful serenity of our meditation area is a great place to start. But then you leave the house and get stuck in traffic, late to work (again). Or your car breaks down on your way to an important appointment. Or you get to work Monday morning and feel stressed by your colleagues, customers, or boss. Or your interactions with your significant other are creating friction. The world around you is not behaving as you would like, and you are not a happy camper—and you might not even know why!

Now is the time to apply these time-tested tools.

Meditation gives us the skill to be aware of our state of mind. Without awareness, we don't even realize we have a problem. We just end up walking around angry or irritable all day.

We now know that our state of mind is a result of our prior experiences, expectations, decisions, and habits we have developed throughout our life.

And as a reminder, what are the habits we are breaking?

Storytelling Habit

We tell ourselves stories (in our mind) about who we think we are and how the world around us should be. We have created a habit of repeating, and taking as fact, our views, opinions, and judgments about ourselves and the world around us.

Those views have been concretized and are viewed as facts through voluminous repetition.

We tell ourselves stories about what the past was and should have been, and what the future will be like or should be: *I am a great father, mother, employee, friend, husband. I am always on time. I am never rude. He/she is rude. I always clean up right away. I am generous. I am handsome. I am ugly. I deserved that job. I should not have financial problems. I am rich. I am poor. People think I'm funny. I dress well. I dress poorly. I have a good ear for music. I am nice. I am not nice. People should be fair. I am always fair. They are wrong and I am right. . . .*

Notice how many times the word *I* shows up in the above paragraph—the dualistic delineation between I and other (everyone and everything else).

The more self-centered we are, the more we are set up to live in negative states of mind when life does not go our way. The world doesn't work the way we want it to—not by a long shot. This leads us to react unskillfully and inappropriately.

We hope you get the point!

Habit of Reacting When We Don't Get What We Want

We react unskillfully when a situation arises that conflicts with our view of our self or the world around us. When we get triggered by situations that conflict with how we think life should be, we react with anger, irritability, jealousy, anxiety, and typically respond unskillfully.

Allowing ourselves to be triggered and our ensuing reaction is a habit. It may have served us well when we were younger, but now it harms us, and usually others as well.

The Tools

Observe Your Breath
One of the best ways to break these habits is also the simplest.

The moment you observe you have been triggered and are experiencing any negative state of mind, simply observe your natural breathing. Observe your breath for a minute or so, without modifying it in any way. Simple observation.

Breathing or refocusing your attention back to the present moment starts to break these habits.

Here is another option. Take three or four seconds to inhale (count inside your mind), and then release your exhale naturally (almost like a sigh). And then repeat. Try doing this type of breathing initially for one minute. Over time you can build up to two to three minutes at a time.

The mind can only be in one place at one time. A multi-tasking mind is a myth. We redirect our mind from the thoughts and emotions we are experiencing to the present moment by observing our breath.

If you feel angry or irritated and you observe your breath for a few seconds, you are chipping away at breaking the habit of allowing yourself to get triggered. As we bring the mind back to the present over and over, we retrain it not to repeat the vicious cycle of trigger, stress, anxiety.

Try it!

Even if you tried this in a previous chapter, now is a good time to practice meditation again. Let's set the timer for two minutes and start to observe. It is one of the simplest and most effective tools for reducing stress or any negative state of mind. So, let's continue to create this wonderful habit, so you can own it for yourself.

Connect Your Breath with Your Body

When you notice that you are experiencing stress, anger, or anxiety, simply observe the feeling in your body where you experience the stress. Identify one spot in your body that is tight or tense.

Now visualize yourself breathing *slowly* into and out of the area where you feel the stress. You can do this exercise for as long as you are able to or have time for. It could be as short as thirty seconds or as long as twenty minutes!

For some of us when stressed, we feel the tightness in our shoulders. Or you might observe your heart racing or your head throbbing. Our neck can feel tight, which automatically tightens the muscles around our skull.

Wherever it is, observe it, and breathe *slowly* into and out of that area. See if you can be curious about the sensation.

When thoughts come into your mind about how to solve the situation, go back to observation mode and continue to use any of these tools. Observe. Breathe in and out of the stressed area for as long as you like.

No judgment. No thinking. Judgment and thinking are not part of the tool.

Try it!

Do a brief body scan and identify a part of your body that has some stress in it. We all have stress in our bodies even if we are feeling okay. So, let's try this simple exercise by finding an area in your body that is "tight," and for sixty seconds, simply breathe slowly, visualizing your breath going in and out of that area. See what you discover!

Gratitude

When you are in a negative state, recall how others in the world are also suffering. Identify the things in your life that are going well. Have gratitude for what you do have—this might include food, family, friends, the country you live in.

Repeating the Four Immeasurables prayer helps reduce our self-centeredness, which is the main cause for our challenging states of mind. Here it is again for your convenience.

May all beings have happiness and the causes of happiness.
May all beings be free from suffering and the causes of suffering.
May all beings rejoice in the well-being of others.
May all beings live in peace, free from greed and hatred.

Everyone suffers at some point—some may have it worse than you, but we all suffer in some way. We can focus on other people who are also suffering and wish them well. This takes the focus off "me" or "I," and the perception of lack that we experience when things don't go our way. It allows us to feel gratitude for what we do have.

Another perspective is to be grateful for the opportunity you have right now to train your mind to undo your habits! Without this experience, how would you learn how to handle this habitual reaction? You wouldn't! This perspective can be a helpful positive reframing of your situation.

When someone cuts in front of you at the supermarket, you can react in many different skillful or unskillful ways to remedy that minor infraction. One way is just to observe your breath and put on an inner smile! Without that shopping experience, you would not have the opportunity to retrain your mind. Thank you!

Be grateful for it. You have the opportunity to learn how to break the habit—the habit of seeing the world through the lens of your attachment to "me" or "I," and the unskillful response that comes after.

After all, they probably didn't cut the line to annoy you. They may be in a rush. Maybe they didn't see you. Maybe they did! It's okay to stand up for yourself, but consider doing it without the negative habitual reaction. This tool makes you realize that the transformation to a healthier mind can be an opportunity.

How much will this make you feel better? Initially, maybe not very much, or maybe a lot. But over time, it can help put a smile on your face, especially when we start to recognize all the silly little things that can get us upset.

Whatever situation you are dealing with, training yourself to be grateful for the opportunity to learn more about yourself is a great way to practice patience, equanimity, self-love, and self-compassion.

Try it!

There is so much to be grateful for. But as life flies by, we just don't remember to express or appreciate those moments. Well, right now you can!

- What person in your life can you think of that you can appreciate now? Silently express your appreciation.

- Recite the Four Immeasurables slowly and with intention three times to really wish the best for all sentient beings.

The more you can express gratitude for others, the more open-minded and less selfish you will be—and the happier and less stressed you will feel.

Self-Talk

We use self-talk to keep ourselves steeped in reality and prevent our illusory stories and reactive responses from becoming our views and inappropriate decisions.

Let's say you are stressed about the future, your mind is going through many worst-case scenarios, and your state of mind is spiraling downward.

Given infinite possibilities of future, ask yourself, how can you possibly predict the future?

Contemplate, memorize, and repeat the following short phrases. If you believe them and have them easily accessible to you, they will help you reset your state of mind back into reality. Feel free to make up your own!

- "I just don't know the future"
- "The past is history, the future is mystery, the present moment is a gift"
- "Not happening now" (a Zen saying)
- "Not always so" (a Zen saying)

Pick one (or all) that you like and repeat them over and over, until bringing them front and center is the new "habit." When you're angry, irritated, etc., one (or several) of these phrases will automatically pop into your mind and help to put the situation in perspective.

Try it!

- Pick one of the short phrases above and repeat it slowly with intention a few times.
- Would you like to try creating a phrase of your own? Try it, and then repeat that a few times.

Now is a great time to start this fresh new habit. We are combating the old habit of repeating to ourselves and believing illusory stories.

Remind Ourselves of Impermanence

Although we covered this topic in chapter 5, here are additional perspectives that can help you when situations arise that are not what you expected.

Impermanence does not mean things will get worse. It does not mean entropy, where everything falls apart. It means things will *change*. For the better, for the worse? Who knows? That will be based on your state of mind and your perspective.

If you focus on the worst-case scenario, guess what? Then things *are* likely to change for the worse or be viewed in your mind as the worst scenario. Who is to say what is a good or bad outcome?

A great Zen story highlights this perfectly.

> The Zen Master Farmer was preparing to harvest his crops when his son ran to tell him that all their horses had escaped from the barn and were nowhere to be found.

The villagers, hearing about this, visited the Zen Master Farmer and commiserated, saying, "Oh what bad luck you have, Zen Master Farmer! All of your horses are gone. You will not be able to bring in your harvest."

The Zen Master Farmer responded, "Good luck. Bad luck. Maybe."

The son ran out into the valley and was able to corral all their horses, and many more that had been grazing with them.

Upon hearing this news, the villagers ran to the Zen Master Farmer and exclaimed, "Oh what good luck you have, Zen Master Farmer! With all your horses plus the new ones, you will have a record harvest this year!"

The Zen Master Farmer responded, "Good luck. Bad luck. Maybe."

While preparing the horses for harvest, the son got kicked in the chest, and was rushed to the hospital for weeks of treatment.

Upon hearing this, the villagers rushed to the Zen Master Famer and wailed, "Oh what bad luck you have, Zen Master Farmer! Your son is injured and now you won't be able to have any harvest at all!"

The Zen Master Farmer responded, "Good luck. Bad luck. Maybe."

Then the country started to prepare for a war with the neighboring country. The government military came to the village to conscript all available young men to fight. In all likelihood, whoever went to war would probably die. Zen Master Farmer's son couldn't join the army since he was in the hospital recovering.

"Good luck. Bad luck. Maybe."

Can you predict the future? No. Can you predict the ramifications and consequences of any action? Probably not. The only thing we can do is do our best to manage our state of mind. Focusing on the worst-case scenario is not only a fool's errand but detrimental to our state of mind.

When you learn to snow ski and you are skiing down the mountain, the instructor tells you, "Don't look at the trees."

Why? Because where you look, you go.

Let's broaden our view of the future possibilities when you feel stressed about the future. Thousands of possibilities *might* happen. Instead of focusing on one worst-case scenario outcome, know that there are many options for the future, most of which we just don't know. How many times has something "seemingly" bad happened, and some good or amazing thing came from it that you never would have imagined?

If you don't want to be surprised or triggered, be open to all possibilities. And you still are unlikely to predict the future. But at least you won't be focusing on the worst options.

Why does this work?

This perspective can break the cycle of incorrect thinking. Incorrect thinking is when we allow our thoughts to trigger the stress event in our mind, body, and speech. Realize and understand that stressing now is not appropriate, given the thousands of possibilities out there. You can't possibly predict the future. But you can predict that things *will* change.

Knowing and reminding yourself of this is very helpful—because it is true! You are not stuck in any one situation. Attachment is based on things going a certain way. Impermanence reminds us that things change, and *not* always for the worse. Just ask the Zen Master Farmer.

Try it!

Think of something that you wanted to happen and didn't. Now you can say the phrase, "Good luck. Bad luck. Maybe."

Let's agree that if what you wanted actually did happen, we really don't know the consequences of that. It may have left us in a worse situation. We just don't know. This helps us keep an open mind about when something doesn't go right. It may still be okay! There may be a silver lining in whatever life brings your way.

Whether something will work out the way we want it to or not, "Good luck. Bad luck. Maybe."

The Conflict Is in Your Mind

In many situations that arise that cause us stress, we stress because of the way our mind is digesting it. Some would say this is the case almost all the time.

We have been trained to blame someone else or blame the circumstances when a situation arises. And those accusations may or may not be true. Regardless, we can decide how we react with our mind, speech, or actions. But certainly in many personal and relational issues, the phrase "the conflict is in your mind" may be applicable.

Examples:

- I don't like the way [fill in name here] spoke to me and I am annoyed and irritated about it.

- I read the news today and got really angry and frustrated with politician [fill in name here].

- I am angry with myself for doing/not doing [fill in situation here].

It is our reaction, our habitual way we view our situation, that is causing the conflict in our mind. In many cases, it is not the circumstance itself. You have the choice on how to react—or not—to any situation that arises. It is up to you.

Next time you find yourself stressing about a difference of opinion you have with your colleague or loved one, *you* get to decide how to react or feel.

Try it!

Can you think of something that mildly irritated you earlier today or yesterday? Great! Now let's own our state of mind.

- Who decided how you reacted in that situation? You did!

- So, decide now how you want to react when that type of situation comes up in the future so you can take responsibility and break the habitual pattern of negative thoughts that arise.

Real But Not True

Tsoknyi Rinpoche, a brilliant, highly regarded Nepalese Tibetan Buddhist teacher and author, tells a story of his experience crossing a glass-bottom bridge in China.

He was going to meet a friend and was about to cross a glass-bottom bridge connecting two very tall office towers in Malaysia. As he got a few steps out onto the bridge, he panicked. He had a fear of heights! He immediately retreated back into the building. As he recovered, he realized that as a Buddhist monk, it would be best for him to "step" into the situation and experience it, instead of shying away from it.

As we all know, with certain fears, this is much easier said than done.

He also noticed how many people were crossing the bridge every moment that he was standing there, without any apparent fear. After all, the bridge had thousands of people cross it every day quite safely.

After he calmed himself, he crossed the bridge, and shared his experience with others.

He found the experience to be an amazing teaching. What he was experiencing was real: real panic, real anxiety. But the reality of it was not true. The bridge was safe. Thousands crossed; nothing bad happened.

As a result of his experience, he teaches the phrase "Real but not true."

While upsetting thoughts are really happening and there is a real biochemistry that accompanies them, they are only representations of our mind's illusory view.

Our thoughts and reactions are often not the experience of this living moment.

Our thoughts are not necessarily a reflection of reality.

Yes, what I am feeling is *real*, but the situation of there being danger here and now may *not* be true.

"Real but not true."

Try it!

Think about a time when you were fearful. It could have been on a plane flight, entering a new situation, meeting someone, making a speech. Even thinking about it now may make your heart race a bit.

Well, that heart racing is *real*, but at this moment, there is no danger, so it's *not* true.

Repeat the phrase "Real but not true."

It comes in handy whenever you *feel* fear but the danger is *not* true.

What Can You Expect from These Tools?

Yes, there are a lot of tools—certainly many more than we shared here. Pick one or two of your favorites and try them out.

We recommend that you start to practice using any of these antidotes on the small irritations or annoyances in life rather than diving in with your biggest challenges at first. Always start with small, unpleasant situations. We don't want to bite off more than we can chew. Over time as you get accustomed to using these antidotes, you will have the skill to use them at the right place, right time, and with the right emphasis.

How do you remember all of these? Find a way that works best for you!

Hang sticky notes on your computer, on your refrigerator, in your phone. Write a journal and refer to it daily. Make these tools your own. And when a situation arises, some of these phrases will rise to the surface of your mind and help make sense of the situation.

One thing you may notice after applying any of these antidotes is that the situation itself may change or shift in some way or another. We can observe that as well. It is an example of impermanence in action.

Simple! (Not easy, but simple!)

In the short run, maybe you will notice improvement, maybe you won't. But in the long run, you *will* see that the stories running around in your mind hold less power over you. The strength and certainty of your (illusory) views and opinions will fade. Your triggered reactions to them will weaken.

Until one day some of those stories and reactions disappear. And then you are free!

Why Do These Simple Techniques Work Over Time?

Many reasons:

- With all of these antidotes, by coming into the present moment, we break the habitual storytelling.

- We weaken the stories going on in our mind that we have been using to justify and judge ourselves and others.

- We break our habitual reaction to whatever is going on around us, or in our mind.

- We bring the body and mind into the present moment—together.

- When we observe our breath, we may experience feeling calm and centered.

- It teaches our body that it is okay.

- We learn that the body can calm itself, even if it's only for a short period of time.

- The breath calms the mind and the breath and mind also calm the body.

- We gain confidence as we attain some degree of control over our mind.

- We recognize that we won't be stressed forever, and that we don't have to be.

- As our mind becomes clearer of challenging states, we now have a more accurate view of reality.

With these antidotes, we learn that reality is not quite as black and white as our mind leads us to believe. There are many nuances and possibilities in how we can view the world. This contrasts with our views and opinions that we tell ourselves repeatedly until we think they are fact.

Retraining our mind to see and experience a world of possibilities on a regular basis encourages us to be open-minded, instead of steadfast right or wrong.

With clarity of mind, we are in a better position to assess if what we are experiencing is a "conflict only in our mind" or needs real action. Outside at night, when it's dark, and visibility is not good, and you think you see something moving on the ground, is it a snake or is it a rope? When you are calm and clear, you are in a much better position to see the situation clearly and deal with it appropriately—if it even requires attention.

These are super-simple techniques, and look at all the potential benefits.

Do these techniques work right away?

Well, the answer to that question depends on a lot of variables from your "habitual" past. Sometimes you will feel better right away, and sometimes not. The important thing is that you are heading in the right direction.

How Can We Maximize the Power of These Antidotes?

To be able to access these techniques, especially when we feel stress, we need to develop our "brain muscles." In other words, these techniques rely on a meditation practice of some kind, preferably a daily or consistent sitting meditation practice.

Doing these techniques in the comfort of a safe space when you have a minor annoyance is easy. Doing them when you are really stressed or angry or extremely upset due to a health or large financial problem may not be so easy. But when you meditate daily, you gain the sensitivity to know how you are feeling, what thoughts are coming through your mind, and what thought or action may have triggered your state of mind.

Many times you don't even know you are triggered, and you walk around angry all day. I am sure we all know people like that—who are just annoyed with the world! With daily meditation, you become sensitive to thoughts and emotions, so you know more quickly how you are feeling and why. And then you will have the confidence and willpower to implement these antidotes or tools.

Many times, when we are really upset or angry, we become attached to our anger (after all, we are right!). *That's my anger, and I have a right to be angry!* And we don't want to let go or calm down.

When you have a meditation practice, the volume of your thoughts starts to recede. You start to notice a gap between some of your thoughts. You are more aware of where your mind is, what it is thinking about, and what your triggers are.

What is the thought that triggered that feeling of anxiety you are experiencing?

Eventually, after establishing a consistent meditation practice, you can see the triggering thought coming. And you can decide where you want to place your mind, what you want to think about, and how you want to react. When approaching a fork in the road, you can choose to go in the direction of less stress.

A daily meditation practice gives us the basic control of our mind that allows us to implement the tools we need. It gives us the ability to work with fear and anxiety to reduce it and weaken it.

In these techniques, we are *not* trying to solve the problem that has arisen. We are addressing our distressed *state of mind*. When our fear or anxiety has reduced and our mind has cleared, that is the best time to "solve" the problem.

Don't have the expectation that any one time you practice an antidote, it will change your world. But over time, with consistent practice, these antidotes will be quite effective.

13

Nirvana/Samsara

Both Buddhists and non-Buddhists speak of reaching Nirvana, as if it is somewhere we can go on the map of the universe. Buddhism does not view Nirvana as a physical place or destination. We can view Nirvana as a state of mind that can be achieved in this lifetime or in a future lifetime.

One short definition we like is that Nirvana is simply the absence of suffering, or the absence of negative states of mind. Nirvana can be achieved for either short periods of time or for a whole lifetime.

Let's be clear that this does not refer to those times in our lives when everything is going our way. As Lama Lhanang teaches his students, "When the food is good and the sun is shining, everyone can be a good Buddhist practitioner." Those times do not classify as Nirvana. That just means circumstances turned out the way we liked at that time. But how is our state of mind when things don't go our way? That is the test of our mind's ability.

Do you want to live in Nirvana or Samsara?

Samsara refers to the suffering, disappointment, and dissatisfaction that sentient beings experience while we are in the cycle of birth, existence, and death. When our states of mind are not in our control and we experience suffering, we are living in Samsara.

Since our states of mind can be determined by us, we can decide how we live—in Nirvana or Samsara!

This example clarifies these two words. Joyce and Dan are trapped in an elevator that is stuck between floors. Joyce decides to sit on the floor and meditate while waiting for help to arrive. And while she meditates, because it is so quiet in the elevator car, she has one of the best meditations ever. She feels calm, clear, and happy!

Joyce is living in Nirvana.

Dan is so angry and upset with his situation. He dashed onto the elevator at the last minute because he was running late. Now he is late and highly inconvenienced. He has no one to blame but himself. He will have to reschedule his appointments for the rest of his day. And who knows when help will arrive. He fumes. He is angry and irritated at himself for choosing that car, at the elevator for breaking down, and at the crew who have not arrived yet. There is no end to his annoyance and no shortage of people, places, and things to blame. His day is ruined.

Dan is living in Samsara.

The Buddha taught the concept of Three Poisons as the source of our negative states of mind. They are greed (or lust), hatred (or anger), and delusion (or ignorance). If we look deeply, these three qualities are the cause of most, if not all, negative states of mind that we find ourselves experiencing. If we can extinguish these qualities, we can extinguish our negative states of mind.

And the antidotes for these negative qualities? They are generosity (for greed), lovingkindness (for hatred), and wisdom (for ignorance).

So should we find ourselves experiencing one of the Three Poisons, we can counteract it with thoughts, actions, or speech with a focus on the appropriate antidote.

Sariputra was one of the Buddha's primary disciples. When he was asked, "What is Nirvana?" Sariputra responded, "Nirvana is the destruction of greed, hatred, and delusion."

Practice

Think about the last time you felt any challenging state of mind—anger, jealousy, pride, irritation, annoyance. Feel how you felt at that moment. That is living in Samsara.

Think about the last time you felt happiness, joy, peace, a calm state of mind. Feel that for a moment. That is living in Nirvana.

14

Mantras

The word *mantra* refers to a sound or phrase that, when repeated over and over, is a meditation in and of itself. A mantra can provide a sense of calm and can also enhance concentration.

In its broadest sense, a mantra can also be a phrase whose meaning allows you to immerse yourself in a new way of thinking about something. For example, in chapter 12 on "Tools to Change Our Habits," we have several phrases, or mantras, that can be repeated to allow us to see the nature of reality more accurately.

"Real but not true."

"Everything is temporary."

"The conflict is in your mind."

The most common mantra in Tibetan Buddhism is "Om Mani Padme Hum." It is a Sanskrit mantra, also known as the Mantra of Compassion.

There are many interpretations and translations for these six famous syllables. A basic interpretation is as follows:

- The first word or syllable "Om" is a sacred sound that came from Indic religions (for example, Hinduism, Jainism, Buddhism) and when repeated can bring one's energy or spirit in touch with the universe.

- The two middle words mean "the jewel in the lotus" (mani = jewel, padme = lotus).
- The last word "Hum" refers to enlightenment.

The symbolism of the lotus flower is important because its roots are deep in mud, while the flower rises above the surface in great beauty. The lotus refers to impermanence, the transitory nature of everything.

The jewel refers to compassion that we develop for ourselves and for others. After all, we are all interconnected, interdependent, and reliant on each other. We all feel suffering. When we realize this teaching, it is easier to have compassion for all sentient beings around us.

This mantra helps us immerse ourselves into the mindset of compassion and the wisdom of realizing Emptiness. They are two sides of the same coin. Deep compassion for others helps us realize we are all the same, all connected, always changing. And an understanding of impermanence leaves us with an open mind about people, views, and situations. That in turn naturally allows us to feel compassion for others.

Here is what the Dalai Lama has to say about the recitation of this mantra: "Thus the six syllables, om mani padme hung [hum], mean that in dependence on the practice of a path which is an indivisible union of method and wisdom, you can transform your impure body, speech, and mind into the pure exalted body, speech, and mind of a Buddha [. . .]"

The essence of the mantra is that Bodhicitta, or compassionate mind, is the precious jewel.

The mantras from the original Sanskrit words were created or "discovered" by great beings many years ago. They were created in such a way that their *sound and energy* resonate in our mind at the same frequency as the spiritual significance intended by the mantra.

Although there is benefit to reciting the following in English, "Om the jewel in the lotus hum," it is limited. By reciting the actual six syllables in Sanskrit—Om Mani Padme Hum—we are connecting our mind with a higher state of universal Mind.

Practice

Now is a great time to try a mantra.

- Pick one from this section and repeat it slowly with intention ten times. If you're unsure about Sanskrit pronunciation, there are many guides online. It probably takes about thirty seconds to recite the mantra ten times. Check your state of mind. Has it shifted in any subtle way?

- You can always make up your own phrase or mantra. Create one now with just a few words of your own. Repeat it ten times slowly with intention. Check your state of mind. Has it shifted in any subtle way?

15

Rebirth

Many, but not all, Buddhists believe in rebirth.

Rebirth means that when we die, "some thing" gets reborn in a new body.

What is that "some thing"?

From a Buddhist perspective, what gets reborn is a part of our consciousness. Another way of saying this is what gets reborn is our karma.

Karma is like a type of memory or tendency. When we do any action (of body, speech, or mind), traces of that action are stored in our consciousness.

When our body dies, and our brain dies, that part of the consciousness continues into the afterlife (known as the "bardo" in Tibetan Buddhism). And then after some time (typically up to forty-nine days), that part of consciousness seeks to be reborn in a physical body. It identifies and is attracted to the parents and enters the womb at the time of conception.

How do we know any of this?

Although this is what great Buddhist masters have taught us for centuries, we know about the afterlife more scientifically from two perspectives.

Many people have experienced Near Death Experiences (NDE). In other words, people who have died (their brain and heart have stopped) have maintained "awareness" of what is taking place in the world of the living. People who have experienced NDEs have come back to life—sometimes minutes, sometimes hours or even days later—and can recount what they "saw" and "heard" in the afterlife. At this time, thousands of NDEs have been documented by researchers and scientists. And it makes for fascinating reading, taking a peek at what we experience after we die.

How does this show that rebirth takes place, though? Maybe when we die, we just stop living, and there is no rebirth or reincarnation at all.

There are also many people who recall the details of their previous lifetime or lifetimes. This happens to some children up to the age of five, after which they forget those memories. Scientists and researchers from many universities and organizations around the world have documented thousands of children who remember their past lives.

University of Virginia's Division of Perceptual Studies has been researching, investigating, and documenting the stories of young children (typically ages two to five) who report in detail their experience in a previous lifetime. One of the many tasks this department of scientists and researchers takes on is researching and proving that their stories existed and could not have been known by the children or their families.

They have been doing this work since 1967 and have identified over 2,500 credible children whose stories about their past lives have been corroborated. There was no way that the child or their family could have had any knowledge about the child's previous lifetime's circumstances.

We recommend reviewing the many videos available online by their director, Dr. Jim Tucker. It is breathtaking listening to their incredible work and to the stories of some of the thousands of children who recounted their past lives.

For those of us who believe in rebirth, depending on our karma, we may be reborn in one of six realms. Here is a brief description of how human beings live in each of those realms:

We are in the *god realm* when we are so proud of ourselves and our positions in life, and we sense ourselves superior to those around us. And we get distracted by the material world and the pleasures it offers us.

We are in the *demi-god realm* when we compete with others to achieve more of "this" and more of "that," and spare no expense to win. We are jealous beings.

We are in the *animal realm* as we fight violently with others (physically, mentally, or emotionally). Countries and people who commit violence are in the animal realm while doing so. The base of their fighting and violence is fear and confusion.

We are living in the *hungry ghost realm* when we keep eating past the point of satiety and at the expense of others who may not have enough food for themselves. Our mind is never satisfied. We never have enough money, material things, love, affection, or success.

We are in the *hell realm* when we are angry and find ourselves yelling at someone, red in the face, fists clenched, heartbeat racing. We are "burning" ourselves.

The *human realm* is filled with desire, doubt, pride—in fact, many of the characteristics found in all the other realms. However, *the human realm is the only realm that gives us the opportunity to reach enlightenment* and leave Samsara, the repetitive cycle of birth, life, illness, and death.

For that reason, and because it is a rare opportunity being born into a human realm, it is a very precious opportunity to live in the human realm. On one hand, we can enjoy much in the human realm, like the god realm. And we also experience much of what is in the lower realms—great suffering.

In the human realm, we have just enough suffering to motivate us to pursue liberation. Too much suffering, and we become immersed in it—with no opportunity, time, or motivation to train ourselves so we can leave the samsaric life.

Many Buddhists also view these realms as a psychological state of mind that we can experience right now in this lifetime. Simply notice how we cycle through these states of mind, sometimes from moment to moment.

Contemplate

Many Buddhists believe that in this lifetime, you were reborn into your family based upon your prior life's karma.

Why do you think you "chose" to be reborn into your family? Although it is not an actual explicit choice, it is nonetheless based on your karma. There are obvious differences between you and your family, of course. But see if you can identify a thread, a similarity in view, an approach to judging situations, or an approach to life that you have in common with your family. It is not about agreeing or disagreeing with them.

If you can't identify this now, then mull it over in your mind for a few weeks or months and see in what ways you have an underlying connection with them or important lessons to learn from them.

16

Who Do Buddhists Pray to?

As we said in chapter 2, the Buddha was not a god. He was a man who, through much effort, became enlightened.

If there is no god in the Buddhist belief system, then the natural question is, who do Buddhists pray to, and what do they pray for?

As in all religions, there are different types of prayers in Buddhism. Here are a few:

- Prayers of aspiration: We aspire to reduce suffering for all sentient beings.

- Prayers of gratitude: We remind ourselves to appreciate what we do have.

- Prayers for good health: We connect with the healing essence of the Buddha for a loved one or another sentient being so they may have good health.

- Prayers for those who have died: We support the consciousness of deceased beings as they go through the bardo and seek a new "life." We dedicate merit from good deeds we have done or prayers we have said to those who die so their future is auspicious in the next lifetime (or heavenly realm).

- Prayers for material wealth: We pray to obtain material wealth, so that we may use it to reduce our own suffering and the suffering of other sentient beings.

- Prayers to remove obstacles: We pray for the removal of internal obstacles in our mind (negative states of mind) or external obstacles that prevent us from helping others.

- Prayers of confession and purification: We confess our unskillful actions of body, speech, and mind. We express regret. We vow not to do it again. And we state that we will perform actions of good merit. We will dedicate that good merit to other sentient beings to help remove their suffering.

- Prayers to protect ourselves: We pray to an aspect of the Buddha, which is a part of us, to protect us from harm.

- Prayers to protect the Dharma (the Buddha's teachings) from being lost: We pray that the precious teachings of the Buddha are not lost or destroyed but continue to exist in order to help others.

- Dedication of merit: After we perform any action of good karma (of speech, body, or mind) we dedicate that good merit to help other sentient beings—alive or dead—so they may benefit from the merit.

- Refuge prayer: When an individual commits to be a Buddhist, they "take refuge" in the three jewels of Buddhism—the Buddha, the Dharma, and the Sangha (community of Buddhists). Taking refuge means we will rely on those three entities, versus relying on money, houses, material things, or specific people who we think can help us. We discuss this in greater detail in chapter 18.

Let's get back to the question of who we are praying to.

In many cases, we are simply reciting prayers that remind ourselves of how we should think, feel, and act. The Four Immeasurables prayer (in chapter 10) is a wonderful example of that.

In addition, in Buddhism we believe that what we focus our mind on, we become. When we focus our attention on the Buddha and his incredible enlightened qualities, that is who we can become (over time).

There was one Buddha, Siddhartha Gautama. When we study his life, we have a chance to become a Buddha too. We can become a Buddha by emulating the qualities of the mind that he developed, practiced, and taught. We are not praying to the historical figure Buddha. We are praying in a manner to absorb and immerse ourselves in his enlightened state of mind.

We can also visualize other great enlightened Buddhist masters. Those great masters live on in our memories. Their great kindness and teachings live on. In this way, they continue to help both us and numberless sentient beings, hundreds or thousands of years later. By "dialing in" to their "frequency," we can connect to their state of mind. And by doing so, we can become more like them.

We can also visualize meditational deities. Meditational deities are characters who may not have existed as human beings. But their enlightened characteristics and personalities are beautiful, compassionate, healing, and powerful. Their stories and descriptions have been passed down to us by great Buddhist masters for many lifetimes. We can focus on and immerse ourselves in their Buddha state of mind and qualities.

By recalling them, visualizing them, and devoting ourselves to that enlightened energy or being, we become inseparable from them and realize that they and we are one and the same. We too have those kind, protective, uplifting, compassionate characteristics in our own state of mind, especially when our mind is not obstructed by self-centered thoughts.

We are not praying to something outside of us. We are connecting to that part of our own mind that these masters or deities exhibit so perfectly. As we focus on great beings who once lived, or on meditational deities who can be described with the characteristics of a Buddha, we have the ability to immerse ourselves in pure states of mind.

Here are two examples of meditational deities that are the most common in the Tibetan Buddhist pantheon.

Green Tara

Tara is regarded as the Mother of all Buddhas. She is an example of compassion in action. She hears the calls of all those who suffer and helps practitioners who chant her mantra to overcome physical or mental obstacles.

Sanskrit mantra: Om Tare Tuttare Ture Soha

Pronounced: om tar-ray too-tar-ray too-ray so-ha

Literal Translations:

- Om Tara, I pray Tara, O Swift One, So Be It!
- I prostrate to the Liberator, Mother of all the Victorious Ones.

Medicine Buddha

This deity is the Buddha of healing and medicine. For example, if you or a loved one has an illness, then reciting a Medicine Buddha mantra would be appropriate. Practitioners visualize Medicine Buddha, or recite his mantra, to overcome mental sicknesses such as hatred, ignorance, and desire.

The Medicine Buddha is "available" to us to heal both mental and physical illness and purify negative karma.

Sanskrit mantra: Teyata Om Bekandze Bekandze Maha Bekandze Radza Samudgate Soha

Pronounced: tay-yata om beck-con-zay beck-con-zay ma-ha beck-con-zay rod-za sa-mood-ga-tay so-ha

Literal Translation: I call upon the healing Buddha inside me and in the universe to remove physical and mental pain and suffering.

A common practice is to recite the Medicine Buddha mantra 108 times with devotion over a glass of water. That water contains the blessings of the Medicine Buddha and may be ingested by the practitioner. This practice can be done daily until the obstacles, illness, or suffering is removed.

Is a real entity called the Medicine Buddha healing us, or are we healing ourselves by focusing on the incredible Buddha nature of the Medicine Buddha? Try it with dedication and consistency and then you can decide.

Some practitioners feel "closer" to certain deities than others. And their meditation practice, mantra recitation, and visualization may gravitate toward their "favorite" deity. Regardless of the deity selected, the most important aspect of deity practice, prayers, and mantra recitations is the devotion one has toward that deity and their enlightened characteristics.

Devotion can be developed over time. And the impact of our prayers—on ourselves or others—is directly related to the level of devotion we bring to our practice as we pray.

Let's also keep in mind that progress and enlightenment is not up to Buddha or your teacher—it is up to you!

Practice

Buddhist prayers almost always include a desire that other beings have reduced suffering. Now that you know that important ingredient, you can craft your own prayer.

- Write down one or two sentences in your own words expressing your desire for the suffering of other beings to be reduced.

- Now repeat your prayer out loud three times.

- Check your state of mind and note any subtle changes in how you feel.

17

Schools of Buddhism

Whether you drink water from the bottom of the ocean or from the surface, it is still salty. Similarly, all Buddhist schools teach the same core teachings.

After the Buddha passed away, his teachings were transmitted orally by his followers to others for many years. As those teachings spread to different countries and cultures, to some degree they were practiced and interpreted differently.

Great enlightened Buddhist masters, who lived centuries after the Buddha, learned, studied, and developed different aspects of the Buddha's teachings. Their own unique style and interpretation were applied to the Buddha's teaching and then taught to their students.

Many refer to the Buddha's teaching as "Buddhism." A more precise term might be *Buddhadharma*—the qualities or teachings of the Buddha. The core teachings, however, are practiced by all schools. And each school emphasizes different aspects of the teachings. This chapter's content could easily fill a large library of books and still not capture all the details, teachings, and uniqueness that each school has to offer.

For the sake of completeness and brevity, we will describe the main schools of Buddhism from a broad perspective.

Theravada

The Theravadin school developed in Sri Lanka from the third century BCE. This was when the Buddha's teachings were first written down from the oral tradition that existed after the Buddha passed away.

The various Theravadin schools tend to emphasize (in some cases exclusively) the teachings ascribed to the Buddha himself. For example, the Buddha's first teachings, the Four Noble Truths and the Eightfold Path, are given great emphasis. Practitioners practice Buddhism to become enlightened and get off the cyclical wheel of life, also referred to as Samsara. And of course, the Eightfold Path and the Buddha's direct teachings are a practitioner's focus as they seek enlightenment.

Mahayana

The Mahayana school started in India in approximately the first century BCE. The various Mahayana schools tend to emphasize practices that will lead one to enlightenment, as they help other sentient beings away from suffering and toward enlightenment as well. Their vow is not to become enlightened until all other sentient beings are free from suffering. The focus of their practices, teachings, and meditation is on universal compassion for themselves and others, and the wisdom that realizes the impermanence of all things.

As far as core Buddhist beliefs, the Mahayana and Theravadin schools agree. For example, Theravadins believe in helping to reduce suffering of all sentient beings, as well as reaching enlightenment. And certainly, Mahayana practitioners believe and practice the Four Noble Truths and the Eightfold Path too.

The primary difference between Theravada and Mahayana Buddhism comes down to how and when the practitioner aims to leave Samsara, the cycle of life and the suffering that comes with it.

Theravada practitioners' focus is straightforward: practice until they can escape Samsara and not have to be reborn again. No more Samsara. No more suffering.

The Theravadin school emphasizes taking care of oneself by following the Buddha's teachings. As we do that, we will then naturally aspire to help others. An analogy is the airplane flight attendant's instruction to put on your own oxygen mask first before helping anyone else. This is for many reasons. Primarily, if you can't breathe, then you certainly can't help anyone else.

Mahayana practitioners also wish to leave Samsara. However, they vow to not do so until all sentient beings are free from suffering. Mahayana practitioners vow to stay in Samsara out of compassion to help others. And only after all sentient beings are free from suffering will they, too, leave Samsara and enter Nirvana. Clearly a high aspiration to achieve, but who said any of this was easy?

And there are yet some other aspects where the beliefs differ from other schools of Buddhism. For example, some

Theravadin and Mahayana Zen schools do not spend a lot of time teaching about rebirth or the afterlife.

Which approach is better? That is not the right question! They are both beautiful ways toward reducing our own suffering and helping others. A better question is which school, teacher, or Buddhist center fits you best?

Vajrayana

Vajrayana Buddhism is an extension of Mahayana. However, it differs enough from other Mahayana schools that we, and many Buddhist scholars, refer to it as its own school.

The Vajrayana school of Buddhism certainly gives credence to and teaches the Buddha's teachings practiced by the Theravadin school. In addition, the Vajrayana masters have developed practices that enable practitioners to reach enlightenment quickly. Vajrayana practitioners believe that enlightenment is possible within a single lifetime. Practices include meditation, breathwork, visualization, deity practice, and mantra recitation to accelerate this process.

Many teachings come from Buddhist Tantric (esoteric) texts, which also include energy body practices and many esoteric methods, best only taught and learned by Vajrayana masters.

Because these practices are esoteric, the importance of a qualified teacher or Lama is essential in Vajrayana.

The Vajrayana path is also known as the "path of fruition" or "taking fruition as path." Our practice and the result we are trying to achieve are the same. We visualize ourselves as the impeccable, limitless deity with infinite compassion now. Our minds mingle with the mind of enlightenment, and enlightened Buddhas. Even though we are not the compassionate Buddha now, as we visualize ourselves as such, we grow into that role, so to speak. And ultimately, we believe that the great Buddhas are not separate from us. They are part of us—inseparable.

As we aspire and act to save numberless sentient beings, we step toward enlightenment ourselves.

Zen

Another well-known Mahayana school is Zen Buddhism. Zen Buddhism originated in China in the sixth century AD and spread to Korea, Japan, and Vietnam.

Zen emphasizes self-control, meditation, and the perception of the nature of mind and the true reality of things. Direct knowledge is emphasized through meditation practice and learning from a Buddhist master.

There is a strong emphasis on living in, and being aware of, the present moment. As one studies with a master, we are able to use them as a model for being at one with all things, living in the present moment.

Pure Land

Pure Land Buddhism is a Mahayana school. In addition to the core teachings of Buddhism already described for Mahayana schools, the focus of practitioners of Pure Land

Buddhism is to achieve rebirth in a "pure land" or Buddha field. A pure land is a celestial realm of a Buddha. A pure land is a realm that is an optimal place to practice Buddhism and to become a Buddha. And since there are many Buddhas, in many cases each with their own pure land, there are many pure lands as well.

As the story goes, the Buddha Amitabha was at one time a monk (or a king depending on the legend) who became a Buddha after countless merit was accumulated over many lifetimes. His pure land is called *Sukhavati* (Sanskrit, meaning "possessing happiness"). He vowed that whoever calls upon him to be reborn in his pure land will be able to do so. When in Amitabha's pure land, they will receive teachings to become a Buddha or a Bodhisattva and be able to help beings from other realms.

The key for calling upon Amitabha is to recite *with sincere devotion* the Nembutsu chant, which means "being mindful of the Buddha." The chant is Namu Amida Butsu, which means, "I take refuge in Buddha Amitabha."

Each person is welcome to choose the school of Buddhism that feels most aligned to them—all of these schools welcome new practitioners. However, we caution against a concept called *Dharma shopping*. Dharma shopping is going around from teacher to teacher, dharma center to dharma center to accumulate teachings. Learning a little from everyone, but not going deep into the teachings or practice.

Although there is nothing wrong in learning from as many people as possible, we recommend that you find a teacher or center that fits you, then devote some time to learning and practicing with that teacher. Better to go deep into the teachings with one teacher and one school than to spread oneself thin with many different perspectives.

We recommend teachers who are trained and are part of an authentic lineage. And of course, they should also practice what they preach. This may take some investigation of your own. If you can feel their compassion, even if they are critical of you, and they lead their lives with an understanding of Emptiness . . . that's a good start.

You will know it when you find it.

Contemplate

What teacher(s) have you had in your life whom you really appreciated or will always remember? In Buddhism, the teacher is the key to opening the door to your spiritual progress.

Here is a short checklist for deciding if a teacher is appropriate for you:

- Are they from an authentic lineage?
- Can you feel their compassion or kindness?
- They may talk the talk, but do they embody the teachings of Buddhism on compassion?

It may not be obvious when you first meet a teacher, but after a few interactions you will have a better feeling about whether (or not) they are your teacher. And you can always reassess after some time. It is your decision. You are free to choose.

18

Taking Refuge

When a Buddhist practitioner is ready to commit to Buddhism, they may take vows, known as taking refuge. These vows are recited in a ceremony led by a qualified Buddhist teacher. When taking refuge, one formally enters the door to Buddhism.

An example of refuge vows from the Mahayana tradition is:

I take refuge in the Buddha.
I take refuge in the Dharma.
I take refuge in the Sangha.

What does it mean to take refuge?

When things go wrong in our lives, most people take refuge in any number of mundane activities or things. A tiny subset of what we rely on when we are experiencing suffering might include watching TV, drinking, eating, sex, drugs, exercise, finances. At those difficult times in our lives, we are relying on (taking refuge in) those activities to get us out of our pain or suffering.

None of these activities in and of themselves are necessarily harmful. However, when we rely on them to help us when we suffer, we are relying on activities or things that provide limited, short-term relief—they are illusory, and as a result, may do us more harm than good.

When we take refuge in the Buddha, we see and understand all that he stood for and teaches us today. This man, through herculean effort, achieved enlightenment, and then taught others over thousands of years to do the same. We can find him inspiring and can rely on him and his teachings.

The Buddha can also refer to other Buddhas who have existed in the past as physical beings or as meditational deities. We take refuge in a higher being, who exhibits all the qualities of enlightenment.

When we take refuge in the Dharma, or the teachings of the Buddha, it means that we rely on the teachings to show us the path to reduce or eliminate our suffering. The teachings expounded in this book would be considered Dharma.

When we take refuge in the Sangha, it refers to the community of Buddhist practitioners. By taking refuge in the Sangha, it means the individuals in the community are responsible for us, and we are responsible for them. We do not go it alone in this world. We are all interconnected and impact each other, as described in chapter 7. As part of a Buddhist community, we are able to be of help to others through actions of body, speech, and mind, and help reduce the suffering of our Sangha members. And they in turn support us. We are on the path together to enlightenment!

By studying the short refuge vows and learning their deeper meanings, we realize that success on the enlightened path is not a solo endeavor. Yes, it is up to us. We all have the chance to be a Buddha someday. But we rely on the Buddha, Dharma, and Sangha for support and to make progress.

Practice

For those of us who are or wish to be Buddhists, you can take refuge in (rely on) the Buddha.

For those of us who are not Buddhists, we can always rely on any higher being.

This could be God, a universal energy, Jesus, Mohammad, a great saint, or great being.

This reliance can be with the god or spirit from any religion where you feel an affinity.

By connecting with a higher being, you allow your mind to rest upon and receive support from that higher being.

Feel free to recite silently or out loud:

"I take refuge in [fill in the name or reference to a higher being here] _____."

Repeat it several times.

This mantra or prayer of refuge is always available to you, 24/7.

19

Vegetarianism

"All beings fear danger, life is dear to all.
When a person considers this,
he does not kill or cause to kill."

—The Buddha, Dhammapada, 129

When a person decides to become a Buddhist or to take refuge vows, it is common to also accept and abide by the Five Precepts that were taught by the Buddha.

They are, in short:

- Do not kill.
- Do not steal.
- Refrain from sexual misconduct.
- Do not lie.
- Do not become intoxicated.

These precepts have been compared to the Ten Commandments in the Old Testament.

The precepts may seem straightforward, but there are many interpretations for all the precepts, which present many possibilities in meaning or intention. One of the most debated is "Do not kill," which on the surface seems simple but can lead to complex questions. For example, what if you kill an animal that is attacking you or a loved one? Even the Dalai Lama has stated, "If someone has a gun and is trying to kill you, it would be reasonable to shoot back with your own gun."

The Buddha did not specify that the first precept was for human life only. He also did not explicitly state that his followers should be vegetarian. Whether or not Buddhists can eat meat is a common question we hear from people who want to learn more about the practice.

With regard to killing animals for food, when the Buddha and his monks were begging for their daily meal, the Buddha advised that monks and nuns only eat animal food given to them if it was not expressly made for them. This direction was applied to monks, not lay people. The Buddha didn't offer direct advice on whether or not lay people could or should eat meat.

It is also important to note that in the process of growing and preparing fruits and vegetables, many sentient beings are harmed as farming takes place. When those fruits and vegetables are sent to supermarkets, the trucks carrying them are killing flies, ants, and other insects during their travel. Even vegetarians and vegans eat food that at some point has harmed sentient beings while it was being produced. It is unavoidable.

Our view is that individuals research the topic for themselves in greater depth. And if one wishes to be a vegetarian or vegan, wonderful. And if one wishes to eat meat or fish, or any food that was once sentient, consider saying the mantra of compassion (Om Mani Padme Hum) from chapter 14 before the meal. In this manner, we raise our level of awareness for the lives that were given for our benefit; and our mantra may in some way help the consciousness of the sentient being, who died on our behalf, to attain liberation. After all, all sentient beings go through the bardo or afterlife as well after they die. They have given their life for our benefit. With the mantra and our intention, we can help them, and ourselves, by praying for their consciousness.

Another beautiful pre-meal prayer that we appreciate was written by Roshi Joan Halifax, an American Zen Buddhist teacher, author, abbot, and activist:

Earth, water, fire, air, and space
combine to make this food.
Numberless beings gave their lives and labors
that we may eat.
May we be nourished,
that we may nourish life.

Consider reciting this before eating a meal. It takes but a moment but can have a great impact on our appreciation for where our food comes from, how it came to be at our table, and how we can "return the favor," so to speak, to others.

Practice

If you eat meat or fish, before eating, take a moment and say, "Thank you for giving your life to give me nourishment." Or use your own words.

And if you are eating fish or meat six times a week, consider eating fish or meat five times a week. By reducing consumption even one time a week, you are now saving the lives of animals every month. Wonderful!

Find the balance that is best for you.

20

What Do Buddhists Have to Renounce?

In the Judeo-Christian religions, there are sins and good deeds. Many practitioners believe you are measured by how much of each you perform throughout your lifetime or at the end of it.

Along the way there are many "dos" and "don'ts" that one must adhere to in order to be a good practitioner. One must give up certain things, foods, lifestyles, and people to avoid sinning. And the interpretation of what one must give up can change depending on which branch of a faith you belong to.

In Buddhism, our formula can be simplified to just a few simple words: *Do no harm. Be kind.* And yes, in the Eightfold Path and Five Precepts, we are taught a few dos and don'ts, but the general guideline that all Buddhists can agree on is: *Do no harm. Be kind.*

And if we are to renounce anything, it is really our desire, or grasping and clinging, to anything based upon a selfish motivation. For example, holding on tight to our strong opinions and views. We can renounce our grasping and clinging to our self-centeredness.

There is no need to necessarily renounce materialism. Owning a nice car and home is wonderful, especially if you can use them to help others. But grasping and clinging to your fancy car, or big house—that can be renounced. Have a lot of money? Great. But holding on tight to it, not being generous, being afraid of losing it—those states of mind are what we are renouncing.

There is no sin in Buddhism, just negative karma when we hold on tight to our things, people, or views. Our self-centered habits of body, speech, and mind generate negative karma—and can be renounced!

As Thubten Yeshe says in *Becoming Your Own Therapist*, "Lord Buddha himself taught that basically, human nature is pure, egoless, just as the sky is by nature clear, not cloudy. Clouds come and go, but the blue sky is always there; clouds don't alter the fundamental nature of the sky. Similarly, the human mind is fundamentally pure."

Contemplate

- What strong opinions do you have (for example, on politics, food, health, behavior, child-rearing)?
- Can you soften those views, and be open-minded to consider other opinions on that topic?

By reducing our strong attachment to those perspectives, we will be more open-minded and less selfish.

Remember, the real renunciation is our desire, grasping, and clinging to those opinions, not the opinions themselves!

21

The Act of Giving

Buddha's teachings are replete with talks and examples that emphasize the act of giving. Many of his teachings, especially to new followers or students, began with the importance of giving and generosity. The Buddha said, "If you knew, as I do, the power of giving, you would not let a single meal pass without sharing some of it." The practice of generosity helps to overcome many mistaken views and habits that we have accumulated, including greed, attachment, ignorance, ill will toward others, and the view of permanence. So many bad habits can be overcome with one simple act of giving!

But simple is not always easy. In the Tibetan culture there is a phrase that roughly translates as "Giving is like pulling hair from your nose." This is obviously a painful thing to do and can bring tears to your eyes. In other words, many times we are not able to give freely. We hold back. It's hard to be generous—a consequence of all of our self-centered habits described earlier.

The first questions one might ask of oneself is, "Why am I giving?" "What is my motivation?" As we discussed in chapter 8 on karma, motivation determines whether what we are doing is generating good karma or negative karma.

Am I giving to help someone else?

Am I giving so I look good in the eyes of others?

Am I giving under subtle pressure brought to bear by others?

The most obvious issue is that whatever materialistic or financial thing we may be giving is ephemeral and can't give us freedom or happiness. In fact, those types of possessions usually do the opposite. We are attached to our stuff! But whatever possessions we have are only temporary anyway.

In Sanskrit, the word *dana* refers to a donation or a gift. It is a type of giving that is done freely with no expectation of anything in return. It also refers to donations that are given to a Buddhist community or a teacher. And although most Buddhist teachings are free and are invaluable, it is appropriate etiquette to make a donation when receiving teachings. It is not a transaction for the teachings; it is simply a show of devotion, support, and appreciation to a teacher, center, or Sangha that helps to spread Buddha's words.

By being mindful before, during, and after gift-giving, we can take note of any of the following:

- Am I giving freely? Am I hesitant?
- Do I want to give more? Less?
- How do I physically feel during the process?
- Am I feeling anxiety?
- How does this gift affect my view of myself? Am I generous or stingy? Or both?

- Do I wish the recipient well? Can they make use of the gift in a meaningful way—even more than I need it?

As we review our motivation and state of mind, we can gently and over time develop a more open, generous nature. We realize that the material or financial gift can help someone, and in so doing help us.

Contemplate

Giving does not have to be something material or financial. It can be giving of your time to help another. It can be as simple as paying attention to someone else when they speak. This simple action may require practice, since often we are busy preparing our response when someone else is speaking. Next time you are in conversation, make an effort to pause and to truly listen with attention. How does the experience feel?

The power of our attention can show love, respect, and support. And it will be greatly appreciated.

Afterword

We are so happy that you have read this book. We know that some of these teachings may feel new to you and can feel awkward. That's okay! Learning anything new may involve some questioning. Questioning is good.

Where do you find the answers to those questions? How do you get clarification or go deeper with anything you have read so far?

Read more. Watch videos. Find a center or teacher. Be discriminating, of course, but also open-minded (remember, being open-minded is good karma!).

Learning Buddhist ways (or any religion, for that matter) is a work in progress for the rest of your life. Don't look to arrive, or get somewhere, or master these teachings. That is not the point.

The point, if there is one, is to just practice.

We hope you are able to continue to put your toe in the water by practicing the teachings that appeal to you. If you feel drawn to some aspects of what we present, then go deeper.

And of course, may all beings benefit.

Acknowledgments

Al Zolynas, for his review and precise feedback in all areas, especially Zen.

Tom Seidman, for his support as we investigated karma together.

Maricruz Gomez and Alberto Garcia, for their accurate feedback on Vajrayana. I am grateful to them for sharing their wisdom.

Bob Isaacson, for his review, outstanding feedback, and perspective.

Cynthia Orozco and Monica Friedlander, for their thoughtful feedback after reading an early manuscript.

Sarah Stanton, for being the best editor in the universe.

Joe Kulin, for his guidance, expertise, and patience in getting our books published.

Resources

*The Heart of the Buddha's Teaching:
Transforming Suffering into Peace, Joy, and
Liberation*, by Thich Nhat Hanh

*When Things Fall Apart: Heart Advice for
Difficult Times*, by Pema Chödrön

The Pocket Pema Chödrön, by Pema Chödrön

The Art of Happiness: A Handbook for Living,
by His Holiness the Fourteenth Dalai Lama

*The Tibetan Book of the Dead for Beginners:
A Guide to Living and Dying*, by Lama
Lhanang Rinpoche and Mordy Levine

*The Beginner's Guide to Karma: How to Live
with Less Negativity and More Peace*, by Lama
Lhanang Rinpoche and Mordy Levine

About the Authors

Venerable Lama Lhanang Rinpoche

Venerable Lama Lhanang Rinpoche was born in Golok, Amdo, northeast of Tibet. As a child, he entered the Thubten Chokor Ling Monastery located in the Gande region, Golok, under the guidance of his root teacher Kyabye Orgyen Kusum Lingpa, where in addition to developing a complete monastic education, he trained in the yogi lineage of Anu Yoga.

He was recognized as the rebirth of Ken Rinpoche Damcho, an emanation of Nubchen Namke Nyingpo—one of the twenty-five disciples of Guru Rinpoche—by the Sang Long Monastery located in eastern Tibet.

He has received teachings from a large number of teachers from the different schools and lineages of Tibetan Buddhism, such as HH Dalai Lama, Fourth Dodrupchen Rinpoche, and Kyabye Katok Getse Rinpoche, among others.

Lama Lhanang Rinpoche is a teacher of Vajrayana Buddhism, from the Nyingma school of the Longchen Nyingthig lineage. In addition to the instructions of Buddhism, he studied history, astrology, grammar, Tibetan medicine, painting, sculpture, music, and theater. All this has led him to share teachings on the proper use of the body, the word, and the mind, with the motto *World peace through inner peace.*

His life in the West has also been dedicated to sharing the teachings of the Buddha through his painting, in which he reflects his relationship with everyday life, no matter where he is in the world. He is coauthor, with Mordy Levine, of *The Tibetan Book of the Dead for Beginners* and *The Beginner's Guide to Karma.*

He currently lives in San Diego, California, with his wife and child. He directs Jigme Lingpa Center, in addition to sharing his teachings in centers in the US, Canada, Europe, and Mexico.

Mordy Levine

Mordy Levine has been a Buddhist practitioner for over forty years. He is the creator of the Meditation Pro Series that teaches meditation for different conditions that affect Western civilization (e.g., stress, insomnia, weight issues, smoking). To date, over 250,000 people have learned to meditate through his series of meditation programs.

Mordy is the president of Jigme Lingpa Center, a nonprofit organization led by Lama Lhanang Rinpoche. The center's goal is to generate benefit to all beings through the dissemination of the Buddha's teachings of wisdom and compassion, in order to achieve a sustainable future of peace and harmony for all.

Mordy has been practicing yoga and martial arts for forty years, almost daily. He also meditates daily and holds instructor certifications in Karate, Tai Chi, and Yoga.

Mordy graduated from Brandeis University with a BA. He attended University of Chicago Business School and graduated with an MBA. He is coauthor, with Lama Lhanang Rinpoche, of *The Tibetan Book of the Dead for Beginners* and *The Beginner's Guide to Karma*.

Mordy and his wife, Elizabeth, live in La Jolla.

About Sounds True

Sounds True was founded in 1985 by Tami Simon with a clear mission: to disseminate spiritual wisdom. Since starting out as a project with one woman and her tape recorder, we have grown into a multimedia publishing company with a catalog of more than 3,000 titles by some of the leading teachers and visionaries of our time, and an ever-expanding family of beloved customers from across the world.

In more than three decades of evolution, Sounds True has maintained our focus on our overriding purpose and mission: to wake up the world. We offer books, audio programs, online learning experiences, and in-person events to support your personal growth and awakening, and to unlock our greatest human capacities to love and serve.

At SoundsTrue.com you'll find a wealth of resources to enrich your journey, including our weekly *Insights at the Edge* podcast, free downloads, and information about our nonprofit Sounds True Foundation, where we strive to remove financial barriers to the materials we publish through scholarships and donations worldwide.

To learn more, please visit SoundsTrue.com/freegifts or call us toll-free at 800.333.9185.

Together, we can wake up the world.

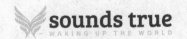